The File
A Mother & Child's Life-Changing Reunion

By
Anita Keagy

Evangel
Publishing House
Nappanee, Indiana 46550

Requests for information should be addressed to:
Evangel Publishing House
2000 Evangel Way
P.O. Box 189
Nappanee, Indiana 46550
Phone: (800) 253-9315
Internet: www.evangelpublishing.com

Edited by Paul McIntire

ISBN-13: 978-1-934233-03-0
ISBN-10: 1-934233-03-X
Library of Congress Catalog Control Number: 2007940734

Printed in the United States of America

9 0 11 12 EP 8 7 6 5 4 3 2

DEDICATION

To my Heavenly Father

Who heard my cry for help and lifted me out of the pit of despair. You set my feet on solid ground and steadied me as I walked along this journey. You have given me a new song, a hymn of praise which I cannot help but sing. May all who read this book be astounded by what you have done and put their trust in you, Lord.

Weeping may endure for a night,

but joy comes in the morning.

Psalm 30:5 (KJV)

Table of Contents

Introduction ix

Chapter 1   Life as a Preacher's Kid 1

Chapter 2   How Far Is Too Far? 5

Chapter 3   Not the New Life I Expected 11

Chapter 4   The Closet Decision 17

Chapter 5   "Doing Time" 27

Chapter 6   Birth Day 35

Chapter 7   Empty Hands 39

Chapter 8   Would I Ever See My Daughter Again? 45

Chapter 9   Surprises, Soap Operas and Scripture 55

Chapter 10   Letters in Her File 61

Chapter 11   The Search 65

Chapter 12   Connecting the Pieces 73

Chapter 13   The Reunion 81

Chapter 14   Becoming My Daughter's Friend 89

Chapter 15   Opening God's File for You 97

Reassurance from Twila 101

Closing Words of Encouragement 105

ACKNOWLEDGMENTS

I am deeply grateful to those who have supported me through the years and who helped this story to have a happy ending:

My family and friends who have walked beside me in this journey and encouraged me every step of the way

Paul, my loving husband and our four children, Shelly, Carrie, Joshua and Ryan

My loving parents, Rev. Gerald and Dr. Lucille Wingert, whose unconditional love and godly lives have always spoken louder than any words

My birth daughter, Twila Sensenig, and her husband, Daniel, for allowing me the amazing privilege to be a part of their lives

The doctors who cared for me during my teen pregnancy: Drs. John Kreider, John May, and Alistair Grant

Twila's adoptive parents, Lewis and Ella Groff, who provided a loving two-parent home and raised Twila to be the beautiful person that she is today

David and Ruth Wadel for providing a comfortable setting for Twila's and my reunion

Family Service for providing professional adoption services and letting me know about the file and letters.

Phil Gascoyne and Jan Kamp who were the hands of Christ to me in completing this book

Chris Cooper and Eddie Smith for believing in my story

INTRODUCTION

Recently a local pastor called to ask if he could use our swimming pool to reward a group of teens after a hard day of manual labor in the intense heat. Everything the Lord has ever blessed my husband and me with we have wanted to share with others, so I was delighted that this man whom I had never met felt comfortable enough to call and make the request. All I knew was that it would be a bus full of teens and that I wouldn't have to do any work. Now, that's my kind of party! My husband, Paul, and my 19-year-old twins, Josh and Ryan, had plans for the evening, so I knew that permitting this group to come for the evening wouldn't bother them.

As for me, I was looking forward to an uninterrupted evening to focus on the final chapter of my book. This book project had been stretched out long enough and it was time to bring it to a close. With one final sweep around the pool to make sure everything was in its place, I headed back inside my air-conditioned house to settle into that writing zone that all writers discover. But before I could get back to my office I heard a knock on my front door. It was the pastor announcing that the group had arrived and he was wondering if there were any last instructions. I briefly filled him in on which bathroom was available inside my house for the group if needed and reminded him to emphasize the "No Diving" rule in our pool since we didn't have a deep end. You could hear the teens walking past our house and down the steps to the pool. Quickly moving to the kitchen so that I could spy out the back window, I started counting the kids. There had to have been at least 40 teens, not counting the leaders! How were they all going to fit in our pool? Within seconds many had jumped in, thrilled to be able to cool off after being in the oppressive heat all day. A smile came over my face as I watched them enjoying life.

Soon there was another knock at my door. This time it was several teen girls asking if I had a room that they could use to change into their bathing suits. I pointed them to the nearest bathroom and then waited for them to come out because I had some questions. Ten minutes later, as they walked through my kitchen toward the door, I asked them who they were and where they were from. These youthful girls explained that they were part of a national youth ministry organization and that they were from many different states. One of their first stops had been Lancaster County and they were busy volunteering in churches and communities to give an encouraging and helping hand to anyone who needed it. The minute I heard them say, "we come from many different states," I knew this was a divine appointment from God. He had seen my heart's desire in wanting to reach as many teens and young adults as possible with His message of love, hope, and redemption – a message that I had experienced through a teen pregnancy and the consequences that followed. Not wanting to miss this amazing opportunity, I told the girls my story and asked if they would be willing to take some of my ministry brochures back home with them to deliver to their youth pastors. Anything they could do to help open the doors for my ministry to reach more teens would be greatly appreciated. Without missing a beat they said, "Why don't you talk to some of the youth leaders that are here tonight and tell them?" That seemed to make good sense, so I asked them to take me to their leader.

She was a beautiful young woman around 23 years old. I introduced myself and asked if she had a few minutes to come inside my home so I could briefly tell her about Joyshop Ministries and show her the materials I hand out free to every teen who attends my workshops. As I shared the story of my unplanned teenage pregnancy with her and how the Lord is now using it for His glory, she became excited and said she would love to tell others about this ministry. I gave her several ministry cards with contact information and then she headed back outside to the pool. Thankful that the Lord had opened this door, I decided that

I had better get back to my office to begin work on my manuscript. As I headed that direction, I heard another knock on my door. It was Michele, the youth leader. She apologized for interrupting me but wanted to know if I would be willing to come out to the pool and share my story with this group. They could give me 25 minutes. Shocked by this immediate invitation yet thrilled at the opportunity, I said yes. With only a few minutes to prepare, I went to the living room and got down on my knees, looked up to heaven and asked the Lord Jesus to use my story to glorify His name. He had 25 minutes to do it! Next, I ran upstairs to grab a large plastic tub that held 50 journal packets. Each packet consisted of a journal, a pocket testament of the Gospel of John, and a highlighter to mark the words of Jesus that the recipients liked. With my stomach starting to flop around with nervousness, I headed down the steps carrying the container.

These teens had climbed out of the pool and were sitting on the cement deck waiting for this impromptu moment. As I inwardly spoke one more prayer for help from God, I thanked the group for allowing me the privilege to share with them a true-life story. During the next 20 minutes, you could have heard a pin drop as I spoke candidly about my past. These teens were so attentive and I could only hope that their consciences were seared as I set them up for the punch line. In closing, I offered them the free journal packets and challenged each person to commit a small portion of time every morning for the next 21 days to God and reading His Words. My heart was beating with joy and excitement as I thought about what would happen in their lives if they took this challenge. One of the youth leaders immediately stood up as soon as I finished and asked if she could pray a blessing over my ministry since she had been challenged by the message and wanted to bless me for that. Graciously, I welcomed her prayer. What I wasn't counting on was the teens' immediate responses when the leader finished. Many lined up to talk and thank me for sharing my story and the divine revelation that God had given pertaining to that painful part of my past. Some confessed sexual sins to me and were in need of godly counsel to be set free. One particular teen told me how she had felt jealous as she would listen to other teens talking about how God had spoken to them and she just couldn't understand how they could hear God. She longed to hear God speaking to her. After hearing my story she finally understood why she hadn't heard God speaking. She hadn't been reading her Bible, which is one of the primary ways God speaks to us! This was a new revelation to her and she was so excited to have this opportunity to read the letter of John in her journal packet and to start on her new journey of listening to God and hearing Him speak! Many of these teens promised that they would take the challenge and hold each other accountable. As these wonderful teens packed up to head to their overnight destination, I felt indebted to God for allowing me the opportunity to speak truth, hope and encouragement over their lives.

Later in the evening my husband mentioned that he and the boys had come home from their activities shocked to hear me speaking around the pool to this group. They chose to sit on the deck out of sight and try to figure out what was happening. As usual when I got to the most difficult part of my testimony tears started coming. One of my sons leaned over to his dad and asked, "Why does mom always cry when she gets to this part?" Paul did his best to try to answer that one but the truth of the matter is that some time ago I asked God to cry His tears through me so that those who hear the message might possibly get a glimpse of His pain to be reunited with His children.

One of my favorite history stories in the Old Testament of the Bible takes place in the very first book of Genesis, chapters 37-50. Joseph was a young man with big dreams but his older brothers were a bit jealous of him and thought he was cocky. His troubles began at the young age of 17 when his brothers got the bright idea to throw him into a deep empty pit until they could decide his fate. Should they kill him or sell him off as a slave to some foreigners? Thinking it best not to murder him, they waited for some

Ishmaelites to come by and they sold Joseph to them for a pretty little profit. Joseph ended up in Egypt as a slave and for years he suffered many injustices and hardships. Surely there were days in his life that he felt abandoned by God and could see no possible way for any good to come out of his enslavement. All the while, God had a plan and was unfolding it. The climax of the story is found in the last chapters of Genesis as Pharaoh puts Joseph in charge of the whole land of Egypt. He saves the land from famine and is reunited with his brothers in a stunning way. The brother's who are fearful of this discovery and assuming Joseph will take revenge on their hateful actions from years earlier, throw themselves down before him and say, "We are your slaves." With words of mercy and forgiveness Joseph responds, "Don't be afraid. Am I in the place of God? You intended to harm me, but God intended it for good to accomplish what is now being done, the saving of many lives" (Genesis 50:19-20 NIV).

Thirty years later, after experiencing that sense of being thrown into a deep empty pit at the young age of 17, I too can shout triumphantly to all peoples of all ages and races, "Don't be afraid of the trying and difficult circumstances that come your way. The enemy of your soul and others around you may try to use it to bring harm to you but God can use it for His good and His greater purposes. Hang in there! Victory is just around the corner and God will use you to encourage others who are facing similar battles. Maybe he will use your life to rescue many others!

My prayer and purpose for sharing this true story is that God will use it to save the lives of many unborn babies who would be aborted otherwise and to rescue the many lives that are in spiritual darkness longing for the true Light.

CHAPTER 1

LIFE AS A PREACHER'S KID

At 17 and a senior in high school, my life was pretty awesome. I couldn't imagine anything bad ever happening to me, because I was a good girl. "Partying" was not in my vocabulary, and I spent my high school days cheerleading, going to Bible study and hanging out with friends. All through high school I was never lacking for dates, and guys would come and go with the seasons. I was not overly academic but my best friends were, so that helped me to feel smart even though I struggled to maintain a B average. My family was close and supportive; I felt blessed to be a part of a loving home in which my parents walked their talk of spiritual and moral values. My dad was a pastor and my mom the church musician at a small church in Tennessee. Both of my parents were musically inclined, and my mother's unspoken dream was to have a *Sound of Music* family—that is, a family that would sing together. Any time there were special services at our church we would have to be the "special music." Weeks in advance practice would begin. Even though we kids were not wild about the idea, we gathered around the piano on a regular basis to learn a new song and try to perfect our performance. Sometimes I actually enjoyed our times of singing around the piano but when the time came to sing in front of an audience I would be somewhat embarrassed, especially if my peers were in the audience. Being a teen and singing with your family did not seem too hip.

Being a pastor's kid had its advantages and disadvantages. I lived right beside the church and could sleep as late as possible before I had to get out of bed on Sunday mornings. If there was a baptism service, I would help myself to a swim in the baptismal after everyone was gone. And, oh my, in my church the communion bread was homemade and I was secretly grateful if church attendance was low on Communion Sunday because that meant that I could have leftovers that afternoon. Of course, our church—being of Anabaptist roots—did not dare use alcohol for the cup. In its place was real 100% grape juice. Our family was too poor to buy it for personal consumption on a daily basis, so communion time was a treat any way you looked at it—unleavened bread and real grape juice the next few days. Another plus was Christmas time. People from our congregation would give us food and soda (including fruitcake at Christmas . . . Yuk!).

Although this sounds grand, the disadvantages seemed to outweigh the advantages.

I could not get away with talking during my dad's sermon. If my dad noticed I was doing a little too much talking he would call me to the front of the church to sit by myself. Sleeping in till the last minute was nice, but I had to be at church every time the doors were open. That meant Sunday morning, Sunday evening and Wednesday night prayer meeting. If there was revival service, we couldn't miss unless we were sick. Sometimes I felt like I heard the same message of God's love and forgiveness over and over. Maybe God thought I was dense and needed to hear it! If my mother couldn't be at church, I was forced into attempting to play the piano as the congregation sang hymns. This was scary, not because I was afraid of crowds, but because I was terrible at it. I would have to pick the hymns days in advance and then practice them over and over until I had them practically memorized. For some reason that did not seem to help, and to this day I can still relive the horror scenes of major goof-ups, like the time I completely lost my place in the middle of a song I'd practiced all week. Feeling confident, I looked up at the congregation like the pros do. I was not as good as I'd thought, because my fingers came down on the wrong keys and I hit every note but the right one. It was impossible to get back on track so the congregation finished singing the song *a cappella* as my father and the people in the congregation did their best to hide their smiles.

Preacher's kids had to set the example; therefore, I was not allowed to go to movies or dances or listen to rock music. This forced me into sneaking behind my parents' backs if I wanted to join in the typical teenage social life. This minor dishonesty never bothered me much except during family devotions which we had every day. By that, I mean someone would read a story from the Bible and then we would pray together. The Holy Scriptures had a way of convicting my deceitful heart. Even though family devotions were at times annoying, mainly because it interfered with my busy social life, it often brought a sense of loyalty to our family. From an early age we were taught about the Bible. We knew it was God's written Word, and that we were to obey it. Participation in family devotions wasn't optional. Every day we were exposed to God's truths in order to help us cope with life in general. We were also encouraged to maintain our own personal devotional times. Every night before I went to bed I'd read my Bible and kneel by my bed to pray. My parents modeled this. I often saw them in their bedroom on their knees, praying. We kids knew that our parent's relied on God for everything. They literally took every trial to the Lord and depended on Him to give them strength and daily wisdom. Watching them taught me to trust God.

I'm not sure if it was because dad was a pastor or that he thought I might have a tendency to be on the wild side, but he and mom had made all kinds of dating rules for me that I, personally, thought were unreasonable. I wasn't allowed to date until I was 16 years old, and then I absolutely had to be home by 10:30 p.m. Any boy I dated definitely had to be a church-going boy. We were instructed only to date guys we'd be willing to marry. As a teen, I could never understand that logic. Who's thinking of marriage at that age? With such ridiculous rules, who was I ever going to date? Their rules only enforced in my mind what I was sure of: my parents were old-fashioned and had no idea what it was like to be a teen in America. Thus, I commenced to do as I pleased—of course on the sly.

In high school, if a good-looking jock asked me out, and I really liked him, I'd go out with him. I'd tell my parents that he was a Christian or that he attended church. If I was unaware of his spiritual beliefs I just wouldn't ask. That way I could say I didn't know. Mostly, I dated guys of similar spiritual beliefs, but now and then I broke the rule. Besides, I wasn't dating anyone with the mindset of marriage.

Sex was not openly discussed in our family, but I had a clear understanding of what was expected of me. Losing my virginity was not an option. That didn't seem impossible, because in my heart I desired to be a virgin when I got married. I liked the idea of saving my body for my husband and experiencing the "big thrill" on our wedding night. In my mind, that was what the honeymoon was all about. However, what became a challenge was how far I *could* go on a date. I didn't dare ask my parents this question because I knew what they expected of me without even asking, in light of the fact they didn't even *kiss* until they were married. I wished they had never told me that, because that just added to my guilt when I would end up making out with some guy on a date.

CHAPTER 2

HOW FAR IS TOO FAR?

During my senior year, I didn't date anyone seriously. Maybe it was because I knew that we would be moving at the end of the school year. Dad had accepted a new pastorate in another state and I had college plans ahead of me. My life was perfect, with a lot of friends, and I couldn't wait to begin a new social life in college.

One real-life soap opera that I was constantly involved in was that of my friends, Allison and Brent. They had been best friends all through high school but Brent wanted to be more than friends. He was in love with Allison but she was happy to keep it a "friends only" relationship. Since I was good friends with both of them, this made me the go-between person. He would pour out his broken heart to me and I would repeat to her whatever he said. Brent and I shared a biology class my senior year. As we spent more and more time together, we slowly ended up feeling an attraction to each other. Neither of us had expected this to happen. So, since he was fair game, I decided to go out on a date with him when he asked. I don't think he had kissed too many girls before me mainly because he hadn't dated too much. Of all the guys I dated, he was the "purest." He was an athlete, clean cut, and we shared the same spiritual beliefs. We kissed, but our relationship wasn't based upon sexual attraction; we were simply good friends who enjoyed being together. We truly respected each other. I wasn't even remotely worried about how far we should go in our dating relationship. The sexual attraction just wasn't there and I felt I could trust him to keep his hands to himself because of his strong moral standards.

One night toward the end of the year, we became bored at a school party and decided to drive around and find a place where we could be alone and just talk. We ended up at a local spot where other dates had the same idea! A common activity in our sleepy town was going "parking." Teens would drive to a dark, deserted area, park their car, and make out. By making out, I mean french kissing, and occasionally exploring each other's body parts. It was so common that you'd often see other people you knew at the same location!

Our talking started off innocently, but we knew where it was going. Talking, kissing, and then the touching. As we were aroused, we went further and further and the next thing I knew our clothes were partially removed, and we went as far as one could go without "doing it." To be honest, I am not sure how far we went. I could feel his body pressed hard against me but I believe there was never full penetration because I was always told that intercourse would hurt the first time and there was no pain whatsoever. There was never any feeling of withdrawal, just him rubbing against me. This is a little embarrassing for me to write so bluntly but it's the fact. If my honesty can help even one person from making the same mistake, it's worth the embarrassment.

There had been times in my past dating relationships that I had played around with arousing a guy, but I had never gone this far. What stopped us from going the whole way was probably our consciences. After the excitement wore off, we both felt guilty. We certainly hadn't meant to go that far. My guilt came from knowing that my parents would be very disappointed in my actions and my conscience told me that God was probably not too pleased, either. Back then, I did not understand that God's moral laws were more about protection than making my life miserable. But in the heat of the moment, all my good intentions went out the window and so did Brent's. I comforted myself by thinking that we at least hadn't gone the whole way. Both feeling that we had trespassed beyond our unspoken boundaries, we drove in silence as Brent took me to my girlfriend's house where I was spending the night.

The next day, we met at the baseball park to discuss our conflicting emotions of disappointment in our actions and yet finding the experience pleasurable. After talking it all out, we prayed together and asked God to forgive us for going as far as we had. In my wildest dreams, I could not imagine that this one brief encounter with sexual pleasure would have consequences that would last for a lifetime. Graduation followed a few days later, and at the beginning of June our family moved to Pennsylvania. Moving day was tearful. A lot of our friends came to see us off, as well as my older sister, Sylvia, who was now married and would be remaining behind. We had our big rental truck packed to the hilt. In fact, my brother, Royce, and my sisters, Judy and Lorene, and I painted a banner on a bed sheet and taped it on the back of the truck. On it we painted a hand with the index finger pointed heavenward—to represent "One Way." And in big letters we painted "Jesus Christ, the Only Way." We thought this would be a cool way to witness while we drove through the different states.

When we crossed into Pennsylvania, we entered a new way of life. We saw road signs with names of towns we couldn't begin to pronounce. We crossed the longest river in the state, the Susquehanna River. I had no idea how to pronounce that. Even the name of the church Dad was going to pastor, Pequea Brethren in Christ Church, sounded strange. It is pronounced "peck way." We kids wondered *what kind of church is a "Peckway"?* The people in Pennsylvania talked with an accent, too. We learned later that they weren't the only ones with an accent. Apparently, we had southern accents and the leadership team warned the new congregation not to laugh at it when they heard it! We had entered Yankee territory and would need to learn new customs and slang words. Instead of "ya" when addressing a group, it was "you-ins"! Everything was strangely different.

In the entire state of Tennessee, our particular denomination had only three churches! Our church was so small we had no opportunity to be part of a large active youth group. Now we were moving to Lancaster County,

Pennsylvania, where our church affiliation probably had 10-20 churches, and Pequea was a large church with a big, active youth group. We kids couldn't wait to be able to hang out with so many other Brethren in Christ teens.

As we turned onto Church Road, we got our first glimpse of our new home. It was a large, two-story white farm house with a red barn beside it. We kids thought this was awesome. We could pretend we lived on a farm. This was my kind of farm living—a barn with no stinking animals or manual labor! Of course, living in farm country had a few disadvantages. We soon learned never to hang wash out on a day that manure had been spread on surrounding fields. We were also introduced to fly strips, these sticky yellow wax strips that you would hang from your ceiling to catch those annoying flies. I would hate it when I would accidentally bump into one. One afternoon out of shear boredom I grabbed a fly swatter and decided to see how many flies I could kill in one hour. Nothing annoyed me more than those buzzing flies circling around my head.

We had only been living in our new home a few weeks when we had to drive to Ontario, Canada, for our denomination's General Conference. It was July and with all the excitement of moving I hadn't paid much attention to the fact that I had not gotten my period the past couple of months. I figured it was probably because of the stress of moving and all the changes taking place in my life. The thought occurred to me, *Could I be pregnant?* but I immediately pushed it out of my mind. Deep down inside, though, I was a little scared because I had always been regular in my menstrual cycle and I didn't think I had been stressed enough to cause me to miss my period.

While in Canada, we went to a Chinese restaurant. I'd never eaten Chinese food before—I thought it was kind of disgusting—and later I threw up. I assumed it was from eating the Chinese food. After a week of hanging out with other teens from within our church conference, we headed back to Pennsylvania and I could now focus on making plans to prepare for leaving home in the fall.

I was planning to enroll at Messiah College in Grantham, Pennsylvania. It was the school my parents and grandparents had attended. There was a sense of legacy and I was really psyched about becoming a college freshman. My mom had accepted a teaching position at Messiah for the fall but she would be commuting. I was looking forward to living in a dorm and being on my own.

At General Conference, I met a young man who was also going to enroll in Messiah College. His father was a pastor, like mine. He was into sports, and I was a cheerleader, so we instantly clicked. We definitely knew we were destined to be a couple and were looking forward to dating at Messiah College. We kept in touch through phone calls and letters and couldn't wait to see each other on campus the following month.

A few weeks after returning home, I still hadn't gotten my period and was beginning to notice changes in my body. Even my sister, Sylvia who was visiting from Tennessee, noticed my breasts were getting larger and asked me if I was pregnant. Fear was creeping up on me but I kept denying it because I thought, *I can't be pregnant. Things like that don't happen to people like me!*

One day, dad and I were driving to my grandpa's house for a visit. It was a pretty long trip, maybe an hour. I liked riding with my dad to places because it always gave us time to talk. I could share almost anything with my dad.

That particular drive we discussed a friend of mine who I knew was probably having sex with guys. It made me feel thankful that I was still a virgin. Of course, dad did not know that I had messed around with a couple of guys and I certainly wasn't going to tell him because I did not want to disappoint him. He and my mom had always loved me unconditionally and I felt some guilt knowing that my actions in private were not in keeping with their standards or God's. In my mind, I just figured what they didn't know wouldn't hurt them.

With college just three weeks away, I wondered how it would feel to leave home and the comfort of their support for the first time. I had no idea that soon I would come to understand the depth of their love and support in a whole new way.

CHAPTER 3

NOT THE NEW LIFE I EXPECTED

August 16, 1974 (age 17)

"Dear Diary: It's over. I'm pregnant. I don't understand it, but I am. Mom and dad are heartbroken. No words to express how I feel. Sick. How will my life turn out? I love mom and dad so much."

Finally, I told mom I'd not gotten my period and that I was afraid something might be wrong with me. I didn't want to tell her but my fears were forcing me into admitting it. I was so sure I couldn't be pregnant, and figured that I would probably need a physical checkup before going away to college anyway.

She asked, "Are you sure you didn't get raped or anything like that?"

I said, "No, nothing like that has ever happened."

Because I'd soon leave for college, dad set up a doctor's appointment for me the afternoon we were headed to a church picnic sponsored by some of the local pastors and their families to welcome us to the area.

Dad drove us to the doctor's office. Mom went in with me while dad sat in the waiting room. The doctor had me lie down on the table while mom sat in a chair beside me.

It didn't take the doctor but three seconds to diagnosis the problem. As I lay on the table the doctor felt my abdomen, looked at me and said, "Young lady, you're pregnant."

The reality of my secret fear being confirmed hit me like a ton of bricks and I could only spit out the words, "I can't be!"

"Why not?" he asked in his authoritative voice.

I said, "Because I didn't do it."

He pointed his finger at me and said sternly, "Young lady, if it's the right time of the month and your vaginal fluid comes into contact with a guy's semen, sperm can swim and crawl and you can conceive."

I couldn't believe what I'd heard. "It's not fair," I thought. I knew so many kids who were sexually active all the time without getting pregnant and all it took for me was one time of getting a little too close. I felt devastated beyond words.

What was my mom thinking? I did not even want to look at her. This was the mom who said "don't kiss anyone until you're engaged" and she is sitting there, hearing this life-altering news of her 17-year-old daughter's pregnancy. In her disbelief she asked the doctor if he was sure. He assured her that they would do a pregnancy test on me just for confirmation, but there was no doubt in his mind that I was pregnant. The two of us walked out past dad in the waiting room to the car. Dad knew by the look on our faces that something was drastically wrong and followed us out to the car. As we got in the car he waited for someone to tell him what was wrong. I knew I was the one who would have to tell him but the words would not come out. Forcing myself to speak, I said, "I'm pregnant." As I audibly admitted the truth to myself and my dad, tears exploded from within.

We drove home in silence, tears being the only evidence that something was drastically wrong. The three of us were stunned and trying to process in our minds this unbelievable situation that my actions had put us in. We picked up my brother and sisters and headed to the pastoral picnic in our honor. Not a word was said to them about what we had just learned. My parents and I put on fake smiles and pretended all was well. At the picnic I put up a front as long as I could, ready to burst into tears any moment. When I thought no one was looking I slipped out of the pavilion, went to our station wagon in the parking lot, curled up on the middle seat and cried uncontrollably. I was so afraid and had no clue what I was going to do or how my parents were going to deal with this.

I wondered what the people of dad's church were going to say. We were the new pastoral family. They'd embraced us so lovingly for these first two months. It was such an exciting time for our family, and I wanted so badly to go to college. "Now what's going to happen?" I thought, feeling sick—sick and desperate. Not knowing what to do, I cried out to God for relief. My answer came quickly. Dad, noticing I was missing, searched until he found me in the car, climbed in, sat down and cried with me. Whatever grief or fears he had, he kept them to himself. If only he would yell at me or tell me what a lousy daughter I was to do this to him. His tears and silence were almost more painful. Yet, in his silence, I knew that he loved me unconditionally and that he and my mother would stand beside me.

That evening my parents and I gathered in their bedroom. Seeing their anguish and tears, and knowing it was my fault, brought me to a new low. Where was I to turn? What were we to do?

> *My child . . . just cast all your care on me; I care for you.*[1]

We did the one thing we knew to do. We knelt by their bed and cried out to God for mercy, wisdom and strength. We brought all our questions and uncertainties before Him, relinquishing control and trusting Him to work things out for His good, even though we felt the sentence of doom.

> *Who remembered us in our low estate: for his mercy endureth forever.*[2]

---

1 See 1 Peter 5:7.
2 Psalm 136:23 (KJV)

Going to bed that night, I wrote in my diary that I felt my life was over. A cloud of fear was hanging over my heart. During my high school years, the thought that I could get pregnant never entered my mind. I was pretty naïve up to my junior year. I had never known the feelings of sexual arousal until I was 16 and on a date with "Bill." He was driving his dad's fancy car, and those leather seats, the romantic music playing in the background and his sexy eyes melted me on the spot. His touch sent chills through my body and made me long for more. I totally enjoyed every minute of it except for the guilt I felt because of my upbringing. There was no turning back. Once was not enough and every date became an exciting experiment to see if we could arouse those same feelings. My only limit was *no intercourse*. I was *not* going to lose my virginity.

You've heard the saying, "Pride comes before the fall." It's true! In my junior year of high school, abortion became legal. Up to that time I had never heard of abortion but its legalization had made it a hot topic at our school. With my self-righteous attitude, I wrote a senior-year term paper on the evils of abortion, never imagining that in less than a year the very thing I spoke out against would all of a sudden become a possible way of escape for me. Now finding myself with an unwanted pregnancy, abortion seemed to be the most convenient "choice."

After all, having an abortion would make everyone's life easier. No one would find out about my pregnancy, dad wouldn't have to endure this embarrassment in his new job, I could go to college, and I'd be spared the sense of shame that can come from giving birth to a child out of wedlock.

Marriage to the birth father was never an option in my mind. Brent was more immature than me, and was only 16. He still had another year of high school. I wasn't even sure how to break the news to him. Since we hadn't had intercourse, would he even believe that he was the father of the child? I did not want to ruin his senior year with this news nor did I want his family to know about it because I knew it would bring sorrow to his mother who had raised her son without a father. Right or wrong, I decided to leave him out of the equation for the time being.

After a sleepless night, my parents and I went for a drive to talk about the decision I was facing. Knowing they would be opposed, I worked up courage to tell them I was thinking about having an abortion. As expected, they were both strongly against it, but in their gentle, loving way, they reasoned with me. They never judged or condemned me for considering abortion. Dad simply reminded me that my conscience was tender. He felt it would be difficult for me to live with the guilt of having taken my baby's life.

My heart told me my parents were right. I really didn't want to have an abortion because I felt I would be snuffing out a life. Sometimes I would feel guilty just smashing an insect unless it was a fly! Maybe an abortion would be different because technically I would not be taking a life because the doctor would do it for me. Abortion just seemed like the easiest way out of this mess I had gotten myself in. My parents explained that the best options for my child were to either keep the baby, and they'd help me, or I could place the child for adoption. It would be my decision and they would support me either way.

CHAPTER 4

THE CLOSET DECISION

Desperate for guidance, I recalled the words of Jesus:

> *But thou, when thou prayest, enter into thy*
> *closet and . . . the Father which seeth thee in secret*
> *will reward you.*[3]

Thinking I had better take Jesus' advice in this bad situation, I went into my tiny closet in my bedroom, huddled up in a ball and began to cry. I was raised to trust God's unconditional love but it was hard to go to Him for help this time. I felt I didn't deserve His help because it was my own fault for stepping outside His boundaries of protection. Not only was I facing the most difficult decision of my life but I now found myself questioning the decision that I had made as a child when I first felt the need for God's forgiveness. A men's quartet had sung at church and something about the words of their song triggered conviction in my heart. I went home, knelt by my bed, and asked Jesus to come into my heart and make it clean. From the time I was 5 years old I believed the words written by John in his Gospel:

> *For God so loved the world that he gave his*
> *one and only Son, that whoever believes in him*
> *shall not perish but have eternal life.*[4]

I didn't want to die; I wanted to live forever with Jesus. I believed in Jesus but there were His words:

---

3 Matthew 6:6 (KJV)
4 John 3:16 (NIV)

> *If you obey my commands, you will remain in my love.*[5]

Because my parents encouraged us kids to read our Bibles, I knew what the Bible had to say about sex. Sexual purity was expected outside and inside of marriage for my own emotional and physical protection. I had chosen not to listen, thinking His rules didn't apply to me and were unreasonable. Did God still love me when I had so deliberately done my own thing, which the Bible calls sin? Would He forgive me for my stubborn attitude of thinking I knew more than Him or was I doomed to hell?

There was only one way to find out. Ask. So I cried out, "Father, I'm coming to you in secret like Jesus taught. Nobody knows I'm here except you. I know this pregnancy is not your Your fault; I brought this on myself, and I'm sorry. Will you You please forgive me and in your Your mercy help me?"

Amazingly those simple words, "Will You forgive me?" brought a sense of relief to my heart. I felt complete acceptance and forgiveness from God and could claim the words of John (see I John 1:9), You have confessed your sin; remember I am faithful and just to forgive and cleanse you.

In that tiny little closet I now faced the hardest decision of my life. I had to make one of three choices: motherhood, adoption or go against my parent's wishes and God's by choosing abortion. Each of these choices had its own set of consequences that I would have to live with for the rest of my life. Whatever choice I made, there would be a loss. In my heart I knew I was not ready to be a parent. At the same time, how could I give up my own flesh and blood? Considering abortion meant I had to answer the questions, "On what day does life begin? When does an unborn child's heart begin to beat?" Logically, I could only answer that one way: at conception. Didn't this life have a right to be born? Did I have the right to stop that child's heartbeat?

---

5 John 15:10 (NIV)

Could I live with taking the life of my unborn child for my own convenience just because the government was giving me the right to choose? What made my "right" to take a life more significant than my unborn child's "right" to live? Ultimately, the fact that I knew there was a life growing inside of me with a heartbeat told my conscience that to get an abortion would mean the taking of a life. Furthermore, if I felt bad killing an insect I couldn't imagine the sickening feeling I would have coming out of an abortion clinic. I now had the difficult decision of whether to raise the child myself with the help of my parents or place this child for adoption. At that moment, a new thought came to my mind. "What would be best for this child?" I had been so consumed with how this was going to affect my life that I had forgotten how this decision would affect my child's life. So instead of focusing my prayers on me I asked God in His mercy to help me and guide me in this decision according to this child's needs and not mine. As I waited quietly for an answer, I sensed God saying to me:

> *Anita, you need to place this child for adoption. I knew this child before you conceived; this life is being knit together in your womb.[6] I will use your disobedience and turn it into someone else's answer to prayer.*

The moment I heard these thoughts whispered in my ear I knew this was the answer God was giving to my cry for help. Even though questions and fears flooded my mind, God's peace settled over my heart. But in that peace there were many unanswered questions such as, "how am I going to face the rest of my family with this news?" His response, "Trust Me." "But Lord, what about all the people at this new church? Surely they are going to judge me and my parents and want us to leave." Again His response was, "Trust Me." "God, I am scared. I don't want to go through this. I am too young to have a baby." "Trust Me, Anita."

---

6 See Psalm 139:13.

Next I pondered the life of this invisible child inside my womb. I boldly ask God, "Who have You picked to be the parents to my child? Can I trust You to put my baby into the best home possible where he or she will be loved unconditionally and be raised in a God-fearing home like I was?" Again He responded with the same reassuring words, "Trust Me on this, too, Anita. I love this child more than you do. I know what I am doing even though you can't see past the devastation of this unplanned pregnancy." Last, I admitted my deepest fears: "How can I be sure that my child will not be emotionally scarred for life by this choice? Will my child feel bitter or rejected? Will my child understand that my greater desire was to put his or her long-term needs before my own?" Could I trust God to cover the emotional needs of this child? Somehow I knew that, with the Lord's strength and my family's support, I would be able to work through this pregnancy and all of its ramifications but I would have no way of helping my child cope with the psychological dimensions of being adopted. This would be the ultimate test of faith. It was then that I had to make the decision to trust God with all of my fears and questions. Either His words were true for every aspect of my situation or none of it. I could either choose fear and carry the burden all by myself, or I could choose faith and trust Him for every minute detail. Which would it be?

Fear seemed easier, but faith was the way I wanted to go. I would choose to trust God with all my heart even though I could not see into my future or my child's. I had read my Bible enough to know certain truths were foundational. If you trust God, He will lead and guide every step of the way and blessings will follow.

Once I settled the issue of trust, I cried out, "Lord, please give me the courage to do what you're telling me because I don't know how I can do it. Right now, take care of how my relatives and the church are going to respond when they hear the news. Most of all, I give my baby to You. I am trusting You to care for my baby and to provide the most wonderful parents You can find. I have no control over all this; from this point on, it's in Your hands."

> *For I know the plans I have for you, plans to*
> *give you a future and a hope, to prosper and not*
> *to harm . . .*[7]

When I finished crying out to Him, He flooded my heart with the sweetest peace. My fears did not go away but I left the closet knowing He would take care of my baby and me. God gave me peace, knowing that He'd keep His end of the bargain if I kept mine. My part was to trust Him with all my heart and not try to figure it all out. If I would look to Him for help He would direct my steps.[8] Having reached the decision to carry the pregnancy to full term and to place my child in the care of others, I now had to face the humbling process of telling everyone my secret.

August 17

"Dear Diary: Told Lorene (my youngest sister) I'm pregnant. I'll tell Royce (my brother) tomorrow. Parents and I decided that I'd have the baby. Called Sylvia (my older sister). Will tell church later. Cried. At least things are settled. Praise the Lord."

Lorene, the baby of the family, was 13 at the time. Because she really looked up to me, it hurt to have to tell her I was pregnant. I hated disappointing her. I couldn't imagine what her reaction would be. But in her innocence she spoke reassuring truth. "Anita, you know this is going to be okay. Remember, Romans 8:28 says that God will work all things together for good for those who love Him."

God comforted me through Lorene's words. Her simple, childlike faith was what I needed at the moment. Like the sunbeams that warmed her bedroom that morning, her words were rays of hope that warmed my heart.

After that, I told 14-year-old Judy who offered her acceptance and willingness to stand by me through whatever lay ahead. Fortunately she did, because over the

---

7 Jeremiah 29:11 (NIV)
8 See proverbs 3:5-6.

next months I spent many a night in her bedroom discussing what the future held. We would often talk into the late hours and it seemed like every time I would ask her what time it was, she would respond, "11:11p.m." This would make us laugh and to this day we think of each other every time we see those numbers on the clock! Being alone with my thoughts at night, fearful of what lay ahead, didn't seem as bad when I slept in Judy's bedroom.

Next I called Sylvia in Tennessee. Since she had already suspected it, she was not as shocked. She graciously offered her support and was willing to stand by me any way she could, even if that meant that she and her husband would adopt and raise my child.

I was particularly close to my brother, Royce. He was a year younger than me—16 years old at the time. When I told him I was pregnant, he was stunned with disbelief at first. Once he got over the shock of the pregnancy and learned who the father was, he offered his loving support. During the months ahead, he would be the one who would encourage me with his great sense of humor!

We were a very close family and somehow this unexpected turn of events was bringing us even closer. Many a night my brother, sisters and I would stay up late talking. Sometimes our conversations centered on my pregnancy and wondering how the people at our new church were going to respond to it all; at other times we just talked about everyday events, somehow thinking that would make our life seem normal.

Amazingly, one night we recalled a conversation that took place in my brother's bedroom when we were still in Tennessee. The discussion centered around our family having to leave all our friends and move to Pennsylvania. We were all disappointed. We kids did not want to leave! We loved our life in Tennessee. However, as we discussed our options (of which there weren't any) we came to the conclusion that God must have a reason for our family moving and we wondered if someday we would look back and say, "Thank you God for moving us to Pennsylvania!

You knew what You were doing." Now here we were four months later saying those very words. We were extremely thankful that God had removed us from a small town where this pregnancy would have been the talk of the town, to my family's discredit. We had left our small town in high esteem and I was grateful that my parents were at least spared that humiliation. Hopefully, news of this unexpected turn of events would stay in Lancaster.

My best friend, Allison, was another story. How could I keep this from my closest and dearest friend? Would it affect our relationship or her relationship to Brent? I knew sharing this pregnancy with her would come as a huge shock and make her sad, yet I also knew she would not want me to go this alone. So whispering a prayer, I stretched the phone cord to my bedroom closet where I could find privacy and dialed her phone number. When her mother answered the phone I was surprised that after having lived in Pennsylvania for a few months I could now detect that southern accent. It made me smile as I asked if Allison was home. As I waited for her to pick up the phone, I sent up more prayers. It was almost as hard to break the news to her as it had been to tell my brother and sisters. As I broke down in tears and admitted my secret, she and I became instantly closer in our relationship. I could hear her crying on the other end. Allison knew that she was the only person I had chosen to confide in and she assured me that she would not let me go through this alone. Not having time to establish a close friendship with any other girls in Pennsylvania, her acceptance and support meant the world to me.

Later, as other relatives learned I was pregnant there were lots more tears, but everyone stood by me with phone calls, visits and invitations to stay with them.

August 20
"Dear Diary: Cried tonight. Depressed. Love mom & and dad so much."

23

Even with all that support, I continually had to deal with my own emotions. The reality of being pregnant had begun to hit me in waves. I just couldn't believe that I was actually pregnant and I cried a lot. My parents tried to comfort me. They surrounded me with love and not once condemned me or said in self-pity, "How could you have done this to us?" They didn't need to say it. My mind was hearing those self-accusing words almost daily. I was most fortunate to have parents who kept any negative thoughts to themselves.

Dad is such a man of integrity that he made an appointment with the bishop of our denomination and told him about my condition. Even though he'd been pastor of this church only a short time, he asked the bishop if he should step down. The bishop said that he didn't feel it was necessary and suggested that dad present the situation to the church's board.

When the church board met the following Monday night, I cried thinking of my parents having to attend this meeting and tell them about their unwed pregnant daughter.

August 26

"Dear Diary: A rainy day. Dad and mom announced I was pregnant. I feel so sick about all of this."

Watching the cars of the board members driving by our house as they left the church that evening, I wondered what the outcome had been. Did they still want dad to be their pastor? Would they think less of me? Maybe they wouldn't want their kids hanging around with me. Surely, they had to feel embarrassment over this unexpected news. Mom and dad came home shortly after all the board members had left and relieved my troubled mind by assuring me that the leaders of the church had received this news with grace and they had offered my parents their support.

The church leadership felt that our Wednesday Night Prayer Meeting was the best time to break the news to the congregation. Not everyone would be there, and it gave those who were more dedicated to prayer a chance to process and respond in a more intimate and personal way. On Wednesday night, August 28th, my family and I were put to the test.

I remember exactly where I was sitting in the congregation that night as dad struggled to deliver his Wednesday night message before he dropped the bomb. I thought to myself, "No one here has a clue how difficult this is for him. He knows what's going to happen within the next half hour." I kept looking at the clock as I fought back the tears, dreading the moment when he would close his Bible and make the announcement.

When it was time, it took him a second to get his bearings. I could tell he also was fighting back tears. I don't remember his exact words. He basically said he wanted to share some difficult news with the church. With that, he plainly told them that I'd found out I was pregnant and had made a decision to place my child for adoption. He acknowledged that we were unaware of this when we had moved to Lancaster and said he was very sorry for how this might affect the congregation. He hoped that the church would stand by us as a family during this difficult time.

I had asked dad in advance for permission to speak to the church because I didn't feel it was his responsibility to represent me. He called me to the front and I stood beside him tearfully saying how truly sorry I was that I'd brought this upon them. We were their new pastor's family and they'd been so kind to us. We were really enjoying connecting with them and their families. I asked their forgiveness for bringing what I felt was an embarrassment on them as a church.

I wondered how the youth group would respond to me, and how the adults would treat my parents. Dad and mom were such godly people, and it certainly was not their fault I was pregnant. I was afraid people would judge and criticize them, but I just had to remind myself once again that this was now out of my control. God had told me to trust Him in everything. My confidence had to be in Him and not me. He would somehow take this unexpected pregnancy and cause good to come through it. How He would do that I didn't know. I just knew God would bring us through this.

CHAPTER 5

"DOING TIME"

Hanging my head in shame and thankful for the tears that were now blinding my eyes so that I couldn't see anyone's facial response to this shocking announcement, I noticed one of the respected deacons, Mr. Byers, coming forward to stand beside dad and me. In his deep, authoritative but gentle voice he said, "Those of you who will stand beside Pastor Gerald, Anita, and their family with your prayerful support, please come up to the altar and gather around them, and let's pray for them."

Dad and I knelt beside Mr. Byers, and to our amazement every single person came and knelt around us in prayer. They prayed so beautifully—many cried. As a frightened, humiliated and pregnant 17-year-old, their gracious response brought healing to my heart. To have people not condemn me but, instead, forgive and pray for me, this was a huge gift! I've never forgotten the love I received and the lesson of grace and mercy these Christ-followers modeled before me and my parents that night. The worst was over. We had told the core group. We knew others would find out soon enough.

September 3
"Dear Diary: I can feel my baby kicking."

The next six months were the longest of my life. Unable to go to Messiah College, I signed up to take two evening courses at a Penn State satellite campus. My parents encouraged me to do so, and it was a good thing. Attending classes a couple nights a week kept me busy and distracted. It also allowed me to earn some college credit while I was in hibernation.

Mom commuted back and forth to teach at Messiah College while I filled my days by cooking, cleaning and helping with small jobs at church. Every day seemed boring and passed slowly. The highlight of my days seemed to be walking to the mailbox and hoping for letters from my dear friend, Allison. She was so faithful in sending encouragement. Sometimes I would receive three or four letters a week from her. Once she even sewed some cute maternity tops for me to brighten up my limited wardrobe. I was looking forward to Christmas break when she planned to visit and was hoping she'd remember to pack our matching pajamas. They were white flannel with big blue polka dots. Would I be able to fit in my pair by December? I could only hope that the elastic in the pants would stretch that far.

With nothing to look forward to, the last six months of my pregnancy seemed like an eternity and I just couldn't wait until it was over. I felt as though I were "doing time." I was often depressed, cried a lot and wished I could be at college. At times I'd feel my baby kicking, and that would make me cry. Every movement was a reminder that there was a real little life growing inside of me and I was slowly becoming more and more attached to the baby.

A dear college friend of dad's, Dr. John Kreider, agreed to care for me until my ninth month, explaining that he didn't deliver babies. Since mom was working, dad took me to every doctor appointment. I never went alone. Sometimes I felt uncomfortable, as though people were staring at me in the waiting room. Dad would sit patiently in the office and after the appointment we often went out to eat. One day he took me to Fish 'n' Chips®. They served hush puppies, a favorite staple in the south! That was a highlight worthy of recording in my diary along with what I weighed at the doctor's office that day, a whopping 130 pounds—a huge gain on my petite 5'3" frame!

I experienced the love of Jesus through so many people in our church as they reached out to our family with practical acts of kindness, such as new mothers offering their maternity clothes to me. These acts were all gifts to me, and I was so thankful for each one.

September 15

"Dear Diary: Another lady from church gave me some maternity clothes today. She'd just had her baby and doesn't need them anymore, so she passed them on."

Often, I would find myself asking how any woman could go through this without having support. In the 1970s there were not the hundreds of wonderful pregnancy centers available to support women who were experiencing an unplanned pregnancy. I felt blessed to have Christ in my life and the support of godly parents, yet I still struggled with loneliness and fears. It was no wonder that years ago, when abortion became legal, some women felt that it was their only option. Without the huge network of support that is available today, they were left alone with their own mixed emotions. I was extremely fortunate to have such supportive parents who encouraged and helped me to take the courageous step of choosing life for my unborn child. They could see beyond the immediate distress, embarrassment and inconvenience to the long-range effect this decision would have on me and my birth child.

September 29

"Dear Diary: I cried today and feel miserable."

September 30

"Dear Diary: I was depressed all day. Cried."

October 1

"Dear Diary: I went to class at the Penn State satellite campus. My English teacher talked to me about my adoption decision. She was very kind and supportive."

October 3

"Dear Diary: I baked mom a birthday cake and had a party. I feel fat."

October 4
> *"Dear Diary: I went to the adoption agency for the first time today. It wasn't too bad."*

Back in the 70s there was no such thing as an open adoption. Lancaster County had one social agency that handled adoptions and that was my only choice. This was all new to me and I did not know what to expect as I sat in the office of the social worker assigned to my case. She asked a lot of questions that centered on what kind of home I wanted my child to be placed in. All I knew was that I wanted my child to be reared in a home by loving parents like my dad and mom. I wanted this child to have the same type of religious upbringing that I had and to be taught the importance of a *relationship* with God over practicing a *religion*. They were glad for my strong convictions because that helped them to whittle down the long list of prospective parents.

November 5
> *"Dear Diary: I went to the adoption agency again and I feel very depressed. The reality of all of this is starting to hit me."*

November 19
> *"Dear Diary: Boy am I glad this day's over."*

November 21
> *"Dear Diary: I just feel sick about giving my baby away."*

Each visit to the adoption agency got harder and harder. Even though I had been so sure this was what God wanted me to do, I continually reprocessed the decision in my mind. As my stomach grew, and I could see and feel my baby move, I became more and more attached and realized that giving my child to someone else wasn't going to be easy. Somehow I had tried to talk myself into believing that it would not be as hard to give up my baby because I had not been in love with the father and we had not bonded emotionally or physically through the actual act of sexual intercourse. This lie I had fallen for was beginning to crumble fast. How I wished there had been someone I could talk to who had been through this to help me process all of these natural emotions I was experiencing. I had to rely mostly on God and my family. Thankfully, times have changed and today there are more support services available for girls in my situation.

During that time, I read a quote that said something like: "Never doubt in the dark what God has shown you in the light." I felt my "closet decision" had occurred when I was in the light. God had given me direction and I was to obey that in my limited knowledge. However, there were times of doubt when I felt darkness in my soul and discouragement in my mind over placing my child for adoption. I would start questioning the wisdom of my decision and had to repeat that phrase over and over in order to get past the normal fears and doubts. That one quote was about the extent of my counseling, outside of my parents and the Bible!

Whenever my emotions caused me to doubt that I had made the best choice for my child, I had to remind myself: "Anita, you know what God told you to do, and you must stick to it." When I opened my Bible to meditate on God's truth, He'd fill my heart with confidence in Him and assurance that He would take care of my child. His words would remind me that obedience to His ways always leads to blessings.

> *Thy Word is a light unto my path and a lamp unto my feet.*[9]

At other times I felt like Hester Prynne must have felt in *The Scarlet Letter*, only instead of the letter A on my chest, it was my large swollen belly that drew attention. Every time I walked out in the public's eye, I felt self-imposed shame.

---

9 Psalm 119:105 (KJV)

That's when I would become discouraged and depressed the most. How does one defend oneself from the self-righteous judgment of others? I longed for forgiveness over judgment. This was a life lesson that I knew would go with me forever. Never again would I judge others for "falling" into sin.

Prayer and God's Word comforted me the most and I learned to depend on God more each day. When I was tempted to listen to that small whispering voice of accusation and condemnation, I would have to rehearse in my mind the words of the Apostle Paul in Romans:

> *Therefore, there is now no condemnation for*
> *those who are in Christ Jesus.*[10]

If self-condemnation wasn't enough, I often found myself worried about the additional financial load this pregnancy placed on my parents. They weren't sure our health insurance would cover my prenatal care and the baby's birth. Again I had to trust the Lord to provide. January 2nd was my last appointment with Dr. Kreider. When dad went to pay the bill, the doctor wouldn't take a cent. It was another of God's gentle reminders that He was taking care of everything. Boy was He enlarging my faith!

For the last month, my new doctors were Dr. May and Dr. Grant. To this frightened, intimidated and ashamed 18-year-old, they seemed old, although they were probably only in their forties. Dr. Grant, who spoke with a distinguished-sounding English accent, sat behind a huge desk in an office that seemed dark and foreboding at my first consultation. I soon discovered that I had nothing to fear, as both doctors were kind and supportive during those last four weeks. I wondered if they could tell how scared I was of going through the pains of childbirth.

As my due date drew near, I cried a lot, dreading the thought of saying goodbye to my baby. How would I do it? Would I hold my newborn in the delivery room or have my

---

10 Romans 8:1 (NIV)

newborn brought to my hospital room and say goodbye before I leave? In that era, seeing your child was discouraged before an adoption. It was recommended that I not bond with the child. What did I know? There were no books or birthparent classes to help navigate me through all of the emotions in making this decision. My struggle to place this child for adoption was so great that I did not trust my emotions. To me, the pain of not seeing or holding my child would be easier to deal with than the pain of having to have my child taken out of my arms. At least that seemed to make the most sense at the time. As worried as I was about going through the physical pain of delivery, I knew the pain of saying goodbye to my child would be a million times worse. As I processed the pros and cons of this decision I decided to opt for not seeing my child. How I would actually do this I did not know, but once again I trusted God to help me at my hour of need. As my delivery date drew near, I grew more and more anxious just to get it all over with. I could have never imagined that the choice to get intimate with a guy one time would lead to so many difficult and hard decisions.

January 1, 1975
"Dear Diary: I'm bored."

The last few weeks seemed to drag. I was starting to get bored waiting for the birth of my child, and I could hardly wait to be skinny again and resume my normal activities. My social life had been on hold for six long months. Except for an occasional outing with the church youth group, I was pretty much a recluse. I was energetic and eager to move on.

January 14
"Dear Diary: I just wish my baby would hurry and come."

January 23
"Dear Diary: I went to see the doctor. I sure hope this is over soon."

CHAPTER 6

BIRTH DAY

January 24
"Dear Diary: I had a bad back pain today. I wish it was time."

That night I started into what I hoped was labor. It was very close to my due date and I was experiencing extreme lower back pain. If this was labor, it was perfect timing! My mom was home for the weekend from teaching and one of my new friends from church was getting married the next weekend and I was so hoping I could go to her wedding wearing "normal" clothes.

As my lower back pain intensified and it seemed that the pain couldn't possibly get any worse, my parents and I made the 20 minute drive to the hospital only to be sent home. It was a false alarm!

Now I was really scared. How was I supposed to know when it *was* time? How in the world could it get any worse? Surely I was going to die from this experience. Enduring the contractions at home as long as I could and hoping that this time the nurses in the emergency room would not send me home, I told my parents that I thought my contractions were stronger and closer together. Once again we made the drive to Lancaster and thank Jesus, this time they told me I could stay even though they considered me in the early stages of labor. How long was this going to take? I just kept praying to God to help me get through this incredible pain.

Fortunately, the hospital staff let my mom stay in the labor and delivery room. They must have seen how scared I was. This was in the days before family members were allowed to be in the room and video tape the entire production. Having her by my bed holding my hand when the contractions got really bad kept me sane. I'd sometimes look at her and plead, "Pray, mom." Over and over again she would bow her head, close her eyes and pray for me while I went through those unbearable contractions.

She didn't care who was in the labor room overhearing her, and frankly neither did I! All I wanted was for these contractions to be over. Finally, after what seemed like eternity I felt the urge to push. The down side of this was that I was told not to push until they told me it was the right time. Just when I thought things couldn't get any worse, they did. How does someone not push when they have the uncontrollable urge to do it? I'm sure I was screaming by this time, but finally I was told I could start pushing. I pushed until I thought my eyeballs were going to pop out of their sockets.

With one last push, my child entered the world and the tears suppressed deep in my heart came pouring out on that delivery table. I closed my eyes tightly and prayed: "Dear Jesus, please help me keep my eyes shut. If I see my baby I won't be able to go through with the adoption."

Dr Grant announced, "It's a baby girl!" I heard her tiny cry, a cry I'd never forget. The hospital staff seemed strangely quiet. Any woman in that room had to have a sense of the grief I was going through. They obviously knew how hard this was for me; so they hurried her out of the room as quickly as they could. Dr. Grant spoke kindly to me as he stitched up the episiotomy. He told me that what I'd done was very difficult and courageous, and he affirmed the decision I'd made. That comforted me as I lay there exhausted in the delivery room.

I reached down and touched my stomach. It was flat. That felt so good. The tears continued as I thanked God that at least this part was over. I was relieved beyond words, but clueless about the intense period of grief to come. As soon as Dr. Grant finished patching me up, the nurses rolled me into a private room that was on a different floor from the women who were going to be able to take their babies home with them.

My brother, sisters and parents spent the rest of the afternoon with me. The following day, I had a lot of visitors from church. Pastor John (a friend of my dad's) from a local church stopped in to offer words of encouragement. He was an adoptive father and wanted me to know how much joy he and his wife had from receiving their own little girl. He affirmed me in my courageous decision to place my child with a couple who desperately longed for a child of their own. Teens from the youth group came and were cracking jokes, trying to be upbeat. I really was happy to have them there; but I was sore, and every time they made me laugh, it hurt!

After everyone left that night, and I was all alone, it hit me really hard—I missed my baby girl. The only information the hospital had given me was my daughter's birth weight. I knew she was in that hospital somewhere and I desperately wanted to go find her. I cried a lot, and asked God for grace to get through this emotionally and physically painful grieving process. I was feeling a deep loss that I was afraid would never go away. Without the wisdom from others who had gone through this process I was left floundering in a sea of raw emotions to sort through by myself.

January 25

"Dear Diary: It was time. Went into the hospital at 7:00 a.m. Baby girl born at 3:18 p.m. She weighed 7 pounds, 13 ounces. Sore and tired. Family came to see me. Praise the Lord, it's over. Very sleepy."

CHAPTER 7

EMPTY HANDS

While in the hospital, the lady from the agency had come by my room for me to sign some papers so they could release my baby from the hospital to her new adoptive parents. When she walked in, I experienced conflicting emotions. One side of me, the selfish side, almost hated her. She'd done nothing to deserve it. In fact she was a sweet, caring person, but it felt like she was taking my baby away from me. On the other side of the coin I felt grateful to her, knowing that she had helped to pick just the right parents for my daughter. Hopefully, she would arrange for my daughter to go straight from the hospital into the waiting and loving arms of a young couple. She was working hard to make that happen and had all the forms she needed me to sign in order to get the permission to have my baby released from the hospital.

Before the adoption agency took my daughter, I asked my parents if they would go to the newborn nursery and see my little girl, thinking that if they would see her, at least they could tell me what she looked like. From the time my parents heard that I was pregnant, they'd prayed for this child every day. For them to see their first grandchild knowing that they might never see her again was hard, yet they were willing to do anything to help me in the grieving process. I'm sure the grief they felt that day as they stared through the window at the hospital nursery helped them continue to pray for her day after day through the succeeding years.

January 28th, the day I was released from the hospital, was the hardest day of my life. There had been no counseling or preparation for this moment. I was left with my own limited coping skills. A nurse helped me into a wheelchair and wheeled me down the long hallway to the elevator. I wondered if we'd pass the nursery where my baby was. Was she still in the hospital or had she been taken to her new home? Why hadn't I said goodbye to her? Maybe if I had, this part of the grieving process wouldn't have been as difficult. A new reality was staring me in the face: my empty hands. Without the gift of open adoption, like they have today, my hands would not have the privilege to hold her. These hands would never know the joy of feeding her or changing her diapers. They'd never be able to comb her hair or wrap her birthday gifts. These hands would have to let go and allow someone else to place her in the loving hands of her new adoptive parents.

Dad waited at the hospital entrance, and when I arrived helped me into the station wagon. It felt awful to leave the hospital without my baby. Even though the physical evidence that I'd given birth to a child was gone, I felt I would never be the same. "Let her cover the mark as she will, the pang of it will be always in her heart."[11] Nothing could be done about the grief in my heart. If only I had had the knowledge to recognize how important it was to say goodbye to my baby, maybe I would have had the courage to hold her and say a prayer of blessing over her life.

I cried for days after I returned home. I missed her terribly even though I felt good about my decision. Sometimes in the process of my grieving I was tempted to blame God but I knew that it was not His fault. Had I paid attention to His commands to be sexually pure, I would not have ever gotten pregnant. Why is it that we think we know more than God or that His laws are just suggestions and don't really apply to us? Why is it that we view His laws as legalistic, to keep us from having any fun, instead of seeing them for what they are: protection because He loves us so much?

Since there were not the multitudes of networks to guide me through this experience, the Lord had to use people from my church! Just when I would reach a low point, He would prompt someone from our church family

---

11 *The Scarlet Letter* by Nathaniel Hawthorne

to stop by and bring words of encouragement. A woman from my church sent a single red rose in a vase with a note that said, "Thank you for respecting the life of your child." Every so often, someone would call to offer a listening ear. Talking about my grief seemed to help me work through the natural mothering instincts I was feeling.

February 3rd was the date set for me to go to the adoption agency to sign some more papers. They weren't the final papers, simply part of the process. That morning I sensed that I would need some extra support to follow through on my commitment to my daughter and her new family so I prayed, "God, I know I can do this but sometimes I feel like I just can't let go of her. She belongs to me. There are times I want to be with her so badly. Please help me to think of her happiness and well-being over myself." I had even named her Shelly so I could pray for her by name, but I never revealed that name to anyone. That was a secret between God and me.

There were times that I tried to think of any possible way to keep my daughter. My parents offered, "Anita, if you can't do this, we'll help you care for the baby if that's what you want." This open door made the conflict going on in my thoughts even more difficult, and the battle intensified in my mind. Even though they made this offer, I knew that they had felt that placing my daughter was the best decision in the long-range scope of her life. Why had no one warned me or prepared me for this intense period of grief? Was this normal? As far as I knew, I was the only person in the world going through this. When would this end? Again, I was left to sort out my emotions by myself but I continued to trust God to be my strength and to meet my emotional needs.

Through all my personal agony, my greater desire was for her to be reared by godly parents, both a mother and a father, and at age 18, how could I know how my own life would turn out? In my mind, this was clearly the best thing for her, in spite of my feelings. That day I called several women from the church I knew would be at home and said, "I know I have to go through with this, but I don't know if

I can. Will you please pray that I will have the courage to sign these papers?" Their commitment to pray for me was a comfort because I knew that I had to sign the papers. It would be so unfair to back out at this stage of the exchange and to ask for my daughter back with the adoptive parents already into the bonding process.

I can do all things through Christ ....[12]

When the time came, dad and I climbed into our little red Datsun, and he drove me to the agency. Once he parked the car, I sat there crying, unable to get out of the car. Seeing my grief was hard on dad. We both wondered when all these tears would end. Finally, I ran out of tears and I told dad I was ready to go into the agency. Every step felt heavy as we walked toward the entry. "Jesus, help me please," I prayed.

Once inside we went into a small office and there was "that lady." I sat down and she immediately told me about my daughter's adoptive parents. She explained that they were a strong Christian couple, involved with youth in their church, and absolutely delighted to have a child. They'd been on the waiting list for seven years. The father had a very good job and was capable of providing well for my daughter. She assured me that they would love my daughter as much as I did.

As the adoption lady shared each fact about these special adoptive parents the Lord had provided, my unspoken fears began to lift off of my shoulders. This information reassured me that God had everything under control and that blessing would come from trusting Him. Experiencing a huge sense of relief, God miraculously gave me the strength to sign the papers.

Dad and I left the agency that afternoon with a renewed sense of hope. A peace settled over me that I couldn't explain. The promise of Philippians was true. "Do not be anxious for anything, but in everything, by prayer and

---

12 Philippians 4:13 (KJV)

petition, with thanksgiving, present your requests to God. And the peace of God, which transcends all understanding, will guard your hearts and your minds in Christ Jesus" (Philippians 4:6-7 NIV). How thankful I was for these words in the days ahead. Anytime I was tempted to worry about my daughter or my life, I would choose to pray about it and be thankful for how God was going to work out His best in both of our lives. My faithful God had already found a wonderful home for my daughter and I believed He would take care of the rest.

February 3

> *"Dear Diary: The lady from the agency promised Shelly would be placed in a good home; young couple, church youth leaders . . . I feel better now."*

As long as I focused on the positive side of adoption I was happy and content with my decision. The thought that there had been a couple praying to God for a child that they could call their own and that God had used me and my daughter to answer that prayer was comforting. I felt good about the fact that I was placing my daughter into a home where she would have a wonderful loving dad from day one instead of having to wait until I found a dad for her. I was grateful that God had given me the courage and the maturity to focus on the blessings of this difficult decision even though I definitely had some hard days ahead.

The last hard day was on Thursday, February 20th. Dad drove me to the Lancaster courthouse to sign the final papers. Once I signed *these* papers, there was no turning back. The room was small, not at all like the large courtroom I'd seen on the Perry Mason television shows. (If you know who Perry Mason is, you are old; if you don't, ask your parents!)

The judge was a tall, distinguished, prematurely gray-haired man. I was not sure what to expect. There had been no books to prepare me for this moment. He asked if anyone had pressured me to place my daughter for adoption, or if there was any financial offer connected with my decision. Looking at me, he said, "Do you know that once you sign these papers you are surrendering your rights to your daughter? Do you truly want to do this?" His questions were like daggers to my heart. Did he have any idea of the courage it had taken to reach this sacrificial decision? Numbly, I answered, "Yes sir." Then he turned to dad and asked if he and mother had put pressure on me to make this decision.

Dad explained, "No, your honor. As Anita and I drove to this appointment I pulled the car over alongside the road and talked with her one more time about her decision. We took time to pray together. She has reached this decision entirely on her own."

With that, the judge ended his interrogation. I knew he was only doing his job. He wanted to be sure that I fully understood that I was giving up all legal rights to my daughter, but his questions reopened my fresh heart-wounds. However, once we completed the legal proceedings, the agony would be over. No longer would I have to wrestle with the temptation to keep my baby.

As the judge placed the documents in front of me to sign, I asked the Lord for courage. Dad watched quietly and prayed for me.

February 20

"Dear Diary: I woke up early, studied my Sunday School lesson, then went to the adoption court. Somehow I lived through it. I had to place my hand on the Bible and swear away my rights to my precious daughter. It was so hard to do. I cried, but God gave me strength."

With the stroke of a pen I had signed away any chance of having any contact with Shelly for at least 18 years. I had no idea how fast those 18 years would fly by.

CHAPTER 8

WOULD I EVER SEE MY DAUGHTER AGAIN?

As time went by, I would at times find myself second-guessing the decision I had made in the hospital not to see or hold my daughter. Had I done the right thing? Would I have had better closure to this deep wound and healed more quickly, if I had done so? Had I missed out on the only opportunity to ever see her? The decision not to see her was probably just my way of protecting myself from being able to spot her in someone's arms in a mall someday. If I didn't know what she looked like, then my imagination could never deceive me. I was hoping at least to avoid the problem of seeing a woman with a baby that looked the same age as mine and wondering, "Is that my child?" Yet in the aftermath of that decision, I now realize how important saying goodbye is. I know it would have helped significantly in working through the grieving process.

Months after signing the legal documents, some friends from Tennessee came to visit during their spring break. They knew nothing about the pregnancy. Spending time with Jim and Ray made me miss my friends and so I decided to make the trip back to Tennessee with them. Driving down Interstate 81 South I decided to tell them about the journey I had been on the previous months. They wondered if I had ever told Brent about the pregnancy and I said no. It was during this trip that I made the decision to look up Brent. Not sure how to tell him I asked God for wisdom. Once in town I called Brent and we planned to get together the following day at the same ball park where we had prayed months earlier. With no romantic attraction between us, it seemed easier to tell him about the consequences of our brief sexual encounter. Shocked that I could have gotten pregnant he seemed to accept it without showing much emotion. At least he believed me and my conscience was clear after keeping this secret from him for so long. We decided that there was no reason not to continue our friendship and we parted ways.

Telling him was the final closure. I could return to Pennsylvania and get ready for my first summer job, as a lifeguard at our church camp. Brent could finish high school and go on to college as he had planned. He and Allison actually ended up attending the same college and getting married shortly after their graduation.

The summer of 1975 flew by as I spent those months in the beautiful mountains of Lebanon, Pennsylvania, working at Kenbrook Bible Camp. The young campers seemed to enjoy me as much as I enjoyed them and I made many new friends on staff that would be attending Messiah College in the fall. Before I knew it, August had arrived and it was time to pack for school and leave my past behind. I had survived with the help of God, my family, and my friends and had full confidence in my future.

As I settled in to dorm living and a new social life, I never hid my experience from others and remained open to help anyone else who might have to go through a similar situation. Everything I had learned the past months had brought a new level of maturity. Yes, I had gone through a painful time but I felt like my experience had taught me a lot about life—more than what my year in college would do for me. It was great to be at school making new friends and building relationships. Studying was not my favorite activity but I did the necessary work to pass all of my courses.

The following summer I returned to camp where I could enjoy impressionable young campers, sing around campfires, and make more friends. Near the end of summer, I received a phone call from a young man by the name of Paul Keagy. He seemed interested in taking me out on a date. I told him I was busy at camp but maybe we could get together when I returned home at the end of summer. I had only met him once and wasn't sure if I wanted to go out with him or not. After camp, we bumped into each other again and he asked me out. In an instant, a spark ignited between us and I knew I wanted to date this guy. Before we got too serious in our relationship, I decided to tell him about the baby I had placed for adoption. If it was going to affect our relationship I wanted to find out right away! I was so afraid he'd dump me, but he just said that he was sorry that I had gone through that experience and that everyone had a story in their past. We prayed together, and that was that. Sharing that painful part of my life actually brought us closer together.

Returning to Messiah College was more difficult my sophomore year with a boyfriend in my life. We continued to see each other when possible and within a few months I knew that he was the man for me. After completing two years of schooling, I decided that marriage was more exciting than studying and on November 26, 1977, we were married by my dad.

After the reception that night, we drove to Philadelphia where we would catch a plane to Bermuda the next day for our honeymoon. I was nervous about having sexual intercourse because I wasn't sure if I would know how to do it. Friends had told me it would really hurt but none of them had ever had a baby before so I was sure it couldn't be any worse than that! I could hardly wait to get to our hotel room to find out what I'd been missing. I wrote in my diary in the car on the way to Philadelphia.

November 26
> *"Dear Diary: It's my wedding night, and I feel like a virgin. How could I have given birth to a baby and still be a virgin? By God's grace, I am."*

Having had a baby was to my advantage on my wedding night. There was no pain involved, that's for sure! Paul and I enjoyed this new level of intimacy in our marriage and we both hoped to have children of our own in the future. After the honeymoon, we started our life together in a mobile home on the family's produce farm.

Paul worked in the produce business and I worked at a local religious book store for three years. But thoughts of the daughter I had given away were never far from my mind.

At times, I allowed myself to dream about this mysterious person who was part of my flesh. I kept track of her birthdays and would try to visualize what she might possibly look like. Once in awhile, I would let my guard down and allow myself to fantasize about the long-awaited reunion. I wondered what it would be like to meet her and how we would get along. Would she be as happy as I was to be reunited? I tried not to have those thoughts too often, because it did not serve any purpose other than to cause me to miss her. My highest hope was in the fact that I knew she was being raised in a family with the same spiritual beliefs as mine, and I could look forward to the day I would see her in heaven, if not on this Earth. She would always be a part of me and I would never be able to deny her existence inwardly. Even God knew that it was next to impossible for a mother to forget the child of her womb.

> *Can a mother forget the child in her womb.*
> *Even if it could be so, I will not forget you.*[13]

Though I would never forget her, I was determined not to live in the past of all the "if only" moments. I had made a good decision for her and reminded myself that *any* decision I would have made would have had "if only" moments. "If only I hadn't had an abortion, every time I saw a newborn I wouldn't feel this guilt and sadness." "If only I had placed my child for adoption, she wouldn't have to go through this emotional see-saw of wondering which man I date is going to end up being her daddy." It was time to permanently be at rest with my decision and move on with my life.

In our second year of marriage, Paul and I discussed the timing of having our own child. We both wanted to have children but we also wanted to be prepared financially for

---

13 See Isaiah 49:15.

this lifetime responsibility. Somewhere along the line we took a chance one night by not using birth control. Really, I should have known better considering how easily I had gotten pregnant at 17. The first month I missed my period I ran to the pharmacy and picked up a pregnancy test. Sure enough, I was pregnant. Scared but excited, I called Paul at market and told him the news. Over the next eight months I grew more and more excited. Having a child of our own was going to be so amazing! "Finally," I thought, "I will have a child I can keep!"

We didn't know if our baby was a boy or a girl because sonograms were relatively uncommon in those days. We were getting closer and closer to the due date and still hadn't settled on names. Then one night, a few weeks before our child was born, out of the blue Paul said, "If we have a girl, what do you think about us calling her 'Shelly'? I really like that name."

My jaw dropped in unbelief that he had picked *that name*, the secret name that I'd given my first daughter and had never told anyone—not even him. In an instant I knew this would be the name of our child if we had a baby girl. Relieved that we could finally agree on a first name, I answered, "Yes, I like that name."

Our little Shelly was born on December 8, 1980. The nurse commented, "Wow, Anita. She weighs 7 pounds, 13 ounces—the same as your first child." I knew that this little girl was a gift from God to love and cherish for always. Now I had my Shelly—one I could keep and take home! This was a privilege I would never take for granted again. As I left the hospital with Shelly in my hands, I thanked the Lord for blessing me with another daughter. No, she could not replace the invisible daughter that I held in my heart, but a little voice within said, "My child, I am giving you back a precious life for the one you sacrificially let go of." Joy flooded over me while I held this little pink bundle of life.

Like all new moms, this journey seemed new and almost magical to me. I was exhausted from sleepless nights but delighted by the company of this precious life. Learning to nurse and bathe this new life was scary and I was glad that she wasn't aware of my inexperience and some of the insecurities I felt as a new mom.

Eighteen months later I got pregnant again. This pregnancy came as a surprise and I was not jumping up and down about adding a new member to our clan at this point. Once I adjusted to the idea, I accepted it and was disappointed when I miscarried two months later. Strangely, it made me want to get pregnant again. Shortly after that, we tried again and our second daughter, Carrie, was born on December 24, 1983. She was beautiful with peach fuzz hair and what appeared to be blue eyes. Once again, God had blessed Paul and me with another beautiful daughter. As we drove home with our second daughter to our small two-bedroom mobile home, I was grateful for this amazing opportunity to be a mother once again. We had put a baby crib in Shelly's bedroom and the two girls shared a bedroom for the next seven years. I was appreciative to Paul that he allowed me the opportunity to stay at home with my girls. He knew that I did not want to miss anything as they were growing up.

In some ways, having children of my own made losing my first daughter more painful. I'd thought I was beyond that, since I'd experienced so many blessings with my decision to place my first daughter for adoption, but as I watched Shelly and Carrie grow, cut their first teeth, take their first steps, and say their first words, I was reminded of the immense joy I'd missed—and what I'd given up. Would I continue to have this feeling deep in my gut of missing her at times as I watched my children play? To make matters worse, condemning thoughts would heap guilt on me, as the old accusations from the past would resurface: "How could you have given up your own flesh and blood? What kind of mother gives up her own child? Your daughter will resent you the rest of her life."

Any time these battles of the mind would resurface, I would remind myself of the truth of my decision. Yes, I was missing the moments of her childhood but she was bringing joy to her parents. I trusted that her adoptive parents would do their best to explain that my decision to place her was out of love and I trusted God to protect her emotionally. In my heart I knew God would take care of every single detail of all of our lives.

> *Let not your heart be troubled. Trust in God;*
> *trust also in me.*[14]

January 17, 1984

"Dear Diary: Called Family Services to update my records in case my first child ever wants to find out who her birth mother is. To my surprise the adoptive parents had written me two letters to let me know how she is doing. Made me cry—so happy to know the Lord is still keeping His hands on all parties involved! The agency is mailing me the letters. Can't wait to receive them."

It was Sunday, January 16, ten years after giving up my baby that God began to put into place a plan that would eventually reunite my daughter and me. My Sunday School teacher gave our class an assignment. He said, "I want each of you to ask God to show you His love in a new way this week."

As I lay in bed that night, I remembered what my teacher had told us to do. So I prayed, "God, You have been so good to me. You've shown me Your love every single day. I can hardly imagine that You would have a brand new way to show Your love to me, but in faith I will ask You anyway."

Then I fell asleep.

The next morning I awoke with the thought, "You really ought to call the adoption agency and update your records because you've never told them your married name, or your current address. If you want 'Shelly' to find you, you'd better make it as easy as possible." Anything I could

---

14 John 14:1 (NIV)

do to improve my chances of being a part of my daughter's life again was worth doing.

So I called the agency to update my records. The lady took my information and we hung up.

Within a few minutes she called back and said, "Anita, I wasn't sure a moment ago, and I didn't want to tell you until I checked, but we have two notes for you from your birth daughter's adoptive mother. The rule says we can only tell you if you call. I'll put them in the mail to you today."

Receiving those two brief notes from my daughter's adoptive mother was a wonderful "love gift" from the Father. I was overcome with joy from this unexpected information about my daughter. These notes contained my first information about her. Her parents wanted to assure me that she was being raised in a godly home, and they thanked me for giving them such a wonderful girl.

The first note was written when my daughter was about seven years old.

> *Dear Birth Parent,*
> *Just a short note to let you know the child you gave birth to is doing fine. We love, care for and appreciate her very much. She is a <u>wonderful</u> girl! Thank you for her life.*
> *Signed, Her adoptive parents*

Three years later ...

> *Dear Birth Parent,*
> *When we receive a new baby through adoption, it always brings a fresh realization to mind that someone made a big sacrifice for us. We wish to say "thank you" and may God grant you the assurance that you made the right decision. Our daughter, your birth child, is doing fine. She is as a rosebud getting ready to develop into a beautiful rose. Thus far, she has accepted adoption as a way of life. We trust she will continue to feel this was God's plan for her life.*

This note led me to believe that my daughter now had adoptive siblings. Her family was growing just as mine had.

In my initial phone call to the agency I also learned something I'd never known before. I too could start a file for my daughter and fill it with letters, just as her adoptive mother had put the two notes in mine. When she turned 18, my daughter could legally ask for her file by contacting the agency. Stunned by this new piece of information, I had new hope for my dream of a possible reunion. There was no guarantee that she would request her file, but it was worth the effort. All I knew was that I wanted to have letters and pictures waiting for her should she decide to check into her adoption records. I could only pray that she would want to find me some day! Could it be that these files were the baby steps leading up to the open adoptions we have today?

January 20, 1984

"Dear Diary: Received the two notes in the mail from my first child's adoptive mom. Very short but sweet. It's still like a dream. I get this feeling that someday maybe I'll get to meet her. But that's all in the Lord's hands."

After I received the notes, I was tempted to call the agency on a regular basis in hope that there would be another note waiting for me, but I knew that was only wishful thinking. I disciplined myself to call only once a year, and it was seven long years until I received the next note. In the meantime, if I saw a newspaper article regarding adoption or adoption law I'd cut it out and save it. I wanted to make sure that I knew what rights she and I had, since the laws were changing.

As much as I wanted to let her know about me, every time I'd sit down to write her, I'd run into writer's block. I was at a loss to know what to say. What do I say to a daughter I've never seen or held? How do I begin to express the feelings I have for her? How do I explain why I placed her for adoption? Would she believe that I loved her?

CHAPTER 9

SURPRISES, SOAP OPERAS AND SCRIPTURE

Although my husband and I didn't take any permanent measures to prevent pregnancy, Paul and I concluded we were finished building our family. Going through a second miscarriage after Carrie's birth had taken its toll, and with my husband's long hours it seemed to make the most sense to end that chapter of our life.

But God had other ideas and a sense of humor, as well. Two years later I found myself pregnant again. Although unexpected, once we got over the shock, we were happy about it. However, we didn't announce the pregnancy until I was safely past the miscarriage mark. At three months, I was beginning to show. I had heard that with each pregnancy you start showing earlier. Since this was my fourth pregnancy to go full term, I just figured my size was normal.

Six months into my pregnancy another mom asked me, "Anita, you're really big for six months. Are you sure you aren't carrying twins?"

I laughed and said, "I'm sure I'm not having twins. The Lord wouldn't do that to me. He knows I could *never* handle that."

A week later a sonogram revealed that I was indeed expecting twins. As the technician showed us pictures of Baby A and Baby B, Paul looked at me in disbelief and apologized! He knew that his busy schedule kept him from being able to help me much with the kids and house maintenance. He felt really bad trying to comprehend what this would mean for us as a family. Shelly and Carrie were in the room with us. They couldn't have cared less about twins, they just wanted to get out of that small examining room! As surprising and scary as this news was to us, it turned out to be a blessing in disguise. This double blessing would keep me busy for years! December seemed to be our magical month and on the 18th, I gave birth to two healthy boys, Joshua and Ryan. My claim to fame was their birth weight. Joshua weighed in at eight pounds and Ryan at six pounds, 14 ounces—almost 15 pounds of babies! Coming home from the hospital with twins was one of the scariest days of my life. I entered the world of sleepless nights where my days and nights just ran together. My previous disciplined and organized lifestyle faded into nonexistence! Gone were the days of working out at the gym and getting up early to have time alone with God reading His Word. It was all I could do to get to the grocery store, keep up with the laundry, and take a bath.

The only discipline I managed to keep was watching a soap opera, *General Hospital*. Every day I looked forward to the clock striking 3:00. I made sure every kid was taking a nap just so I could have complete privacy during that sacred hour. Before I knew it, I was addicted to the soaps— another guilty pleasure to which my self-righteous self had claimed I would never succumb. Eventually, in my frustration, I realized that filling my mind with that garbage was getting me nowhere. When the show was over I was never happier—only more disenchanted with my life of dirty diapers and a husband who didn't seem to match up to those romantic hunks on the soaps! I needed to get my mind focused on positive thoughts that would make me a better wife and mother.

January 23, 1985

"Dear Diary: I'm starting something new today. Instead of watching my soap, General Hospital, *I'm gonna use that time for prayer and Bible study in order to grow more in my spiritual life. Lord, give me discipline to keep this up."*

The only place I knew I could go for safe and solid advice was the Bible. Those words brought life to my spirit.

Yet why did it seem that there were always more important things to do? There was never enough time to do something as frivolous as reading. To help me get back on track, I needed some accountability. I began to look for a community Bible study that provided child care and could help me grow spiritually as well as nurture my desire to be a godly mother. I loved my four kids and wanted to be the best mom I could. Most likely, I needed help in the wife department, too!

Through the years, I continued to attend retreats, conferences, classes and other activities that, along with reading the Scriptures, would keep me spiritually grounded and growing. The children were growing up so fast. Raising them on a produce farm brought many opportunities for them to bond. Many a summer was spent in the tomato fields suckering and tying up the tomato stalks. By mid-summer, they would all be picking those famous tomatoes of Washington Boro—Jet Star. Then they would be graded, packed, and loaded on the truck to go to market. Even though the kids complained about the work, they found a closeness with each other due to spending so much time together. Often they would come home covered in tomato juice from having fights in the patch using rotten tomatoes. As they grew older, they would go to market with their dad. My husband and I felt extremely blessed to have kids we enjoyed being around—well, at least most of the time!

As life paraded by, I knew that someday I would want to tell my children about their half sister—the sister they might never meet. I kept putting it off, partly because I didn't know when would be the best age for them to know and partly because I didn't want them to get the idea that they could mess around sexually since mom did. I asked God for wisdom and trusted Him to let me know when the timing was right.

When Shelly was 12 years old, I took her for a weekend getaway to a local hotel with an indoor pool. After a fun time of swimming we returned to our room, put on our pajamas, and crawled into bed. We watched Nick at Nite on

TV as I stalled for time, wondering how I would tell her that she had a half sister whom she would probably never know. After fumbling around for the right words, I finally got it out. I told her how I'd gotten pregnant when I was 17 years old, and had given birth to a baby that I'd placed for adoption. I explained that I did not know where my birth daughter was and that we might never know.

When I finished, she breathed a sigh of relief and said, "Wow, I thought you were going to tell me something serious, like you smoked cigarettes or something." In her mind, smoking cigarettes was more traumatic than having a child out of wedlock! She wasn't bothered at all. Her remarks turned what I'd expected to be a rather serious conversation into laughter.

When Carrie was about the same age, I began to ask God when I should tell her. At the time, we lived in an old two-story log home. One day, I was upstairs ironing clothes in my bedroom, watching *The Oprah Winfrey Show*. Carrie was downstairs in the living room watching the same show. I had heard that the topic was going to be about birth daughters and birth mothers being reunited. How I wished that it was me and my birth daughter on that show! With all those deep emotions being stirred up in my heart, I decided that now was as good a time as any to tell Carrie about my past. Maybe what she had seen on the show would give her a better understanding of the emotional process I had been working through over the years.

I waited until the show was over then I went downstairs and shared my story with her. She took the news better than I thought. Then I found out why. Because she is the only person in our family with blonde hair and blue eyes, there was always a question in the back of her mind whether she was adopted. Even I secretly wondered if I had gotten the right baby in the hospital. If it hadn't been for the fact that I had seen the nurses put an identification bracelet on her wrist at delivery, I might have thought I had brought home the wrong baby. In light of the show we were watching, Carrie was sure that I was about to confirm her suspicion that we had kept her adoption a secret for all of these years. She was relieved to know that we had not kept any secrets from her.

With that out of the way, the boys were the only ones left who needed to know. I was in no particular rush to tell them. They weren't teens yet and I knew the Lord would work out those details as well.

CHAPTER 10

LETTERS IN HER FILE

Four kids were keeping me busy. I loved being a mom and caring for my family. Birthdays were special in our home and always included cake and ice cream. Although I never mentioned it to my family, I always celebrated my first daughters' birthday in my mind. As her 16th birthday approached, I knew the time was coming for me to sit down and write a letter for her file. This wasn't a new thought, but I just kept putting it off because I didn't know where to begin or what to say. Since she was only two years away from having the legal right to obtain her file, I knew I had better get my thoughts on paper soon.

My dad's birthday was a few days before my first daughter's, and I had decided to host a party for him in my home with other family members. After our family had gathered to celebrate and everyone but my parents had left, they asked, "Do you get the morning paper? We want to show you something." Curious as to what this was about, I brought them the paper and watched them scan up and down the back section, looking for something. When they found it, they showed it to me.

They had put a birthday greeting for my daughter in the newspaper. It said, "Happy 16th Birthday to Our Granddaughter." They had the date and how they pictured her now, to be a vibrant Christian young lady. They hoped that she might see it. I was touched by their expression of love. After all, she was their first grandchild and I knew that they continued to pray for her daily.

Seeing the birthday announcement they had published in the newspaper was the final push that I needed to pick up a pen and paper. It was time to write the letter I had put off for so long. As I stared at the blank piece of paper wondering where to begin, the tears started to fall from my cheeks. What could I ever say to make up for the years we had been apart? With feelings of inadequacies to express my heart, I simply began:

> *Dear Birth daughter . . . I knew tonight I couldn't let another year slip by without acknowledging your birthday and letting you know that even though I never had the privilege to see you or hold you there is an empty spot in my heart filled with love for you, and it will always be there . . . I just wanted to wish you a happy 16th birthday and let you know that although I gave up parental rights to your adoptive parents you will still always be a part of my life. I don't tell you this to interfere with your family, but to let you know that if you ever desired to meet your birth mom and her family, we would all be thrilled and happy . . . I trust the Lord for the outcome, whatever it may be.*

I wanted her to know that even though I'd placed her for adoption, I loved her with all my heart and she was never far from my thoughts. Did she desire a relationship with me? I was open to it if she was, but I didn't want to push myself on her.

On her 18th birthday, I wrote another letter. This time I included pictures of my family and me. I wanted to do all I could to make her feel comfortable with a possible friendship. Would this be the end of the long waiting period? The chances of a reunion were so slim, yet there were times I'd dream about what it would be like to see her face.

Even though my life was full of happiness, there were times I would wish that she would get her file at the agency. Somehow I knew that if she would read my letters it might create a desire for a relationship with me. Knowing our family, I was certain that if we met, everything would work out for good. But would she ever ask for the file? Worse yet, did she even know the file existed? I was confident if the Lord wanted us to meet we would on His timetable, not mine.

Be still and know that I am God.[15]

These words played in my mind often over the next three years. With each birthday I prayed that God would move my daughter to ask for her file. Maybe this wait was part of God's plan to help prepare me for the exciting journey ahead.

The conflict in my mind of a possible reunion was ongoing, in part because I knew it was now legally possible. Part of me gave up hope of ever meeting her, while another part of me secretly tried to envision what it would be like. After her 18th birthday, dad asked if I had tried to contact her. I told him I'd thought about it, but didn't feel I should do it. She'd have to look for me, because I didn't know anything about her. Since I'd given up all my rights as her mother, I felt I couldn't make the first move. Besides, I didn't want to upset her or her family.

As her birthday approached each January, I prayed that this might be the year she'd choose to open the file and read my letters. I wasn't preoccupied with it, but my desire to know her and to have a relationship was often in the back of my mind.

This desire wasn't about trying to be her mother because I knew that I had legally laid down that right, but a simple desire to have a glimpse into her life and the life of her family. However, I was very happy and content with every aspect of my life and was willing to forgo my desires if she was not interested in a relationship at this time or ever. My life was with my family and they were my focus. One day I had pulled out my diary from those traumatic days so long ago and re-read what I had written on that fateful day, August 16, 1974. At the time I thought my life was over and couldn't imagine how it could turn out with a happy ending. Here I was, 20 years later, with a

---

15 Psalm 46:10 (NIV)

wonderful husband, four amazing kids, and my life better than I ever could have imagined. I was glad I had not given in to the fears that surrounded my unplanned pregnancy but instead had chosen faith in God and His plans and purposes.

CHAPTER 11

THE SEARCH

Shortly after what would have been her 21st birthday and my dad's 68th birthday, my father and I were discussing how the two of them shared the same birthday month. Dad asked me again if I had reconsidered trying to contact her.

My response was, "I think about it, but I can't, dad. I just can't be the one to do it. In my mind she should be the one to initiate a contact, not me."

"Okay," he'd say, and the topic was dropped. His question reminded me that he and mom loved her, and that they, too, hoped to have the privilege of meeting her. His question also planted the seed in my mind, and I'd think about it, dismiss it, think about it, and dismiss it again. One afternoon as my daughter Shelly and I were on our way to K-mart®, I decided to get her opinion on the subject. We could talk about anything and I knew she would give me her honest opinion. I said, "Shelly, grandpa's suggested that I try to contact my first daughter. Do you think I should?"

She looked at me and nonchalantly said, "Well, mom, yeah, I think you should. Because truthfully, if I was adopted, I'd be afraid to initiate contact with my birth mother for fear she'd reject me."

Not once had I ever looked at contacting my birth daughter from Shelly's viewpoint. The idea that she could be afraid to look for me for fear of rejection was a totally new concept. Hearing Shelly's words was like hearing from angels. In my heart, I knew immediately that God was giving me permission to initiate a contact. As soon as we got home from K-Mart®, I talked with Paul about the possibility of searching for my birth daughter. I had to know how he felt about it and the overall effect it could have on our family. He was open to the idea as long as I could keep it all in balance. His only concern was that I not go overboard in looking for her and that our children would always come first. I had no problem agreeing to those conditions. As a safety measure, I asked him to keep me accountable and to let me know if he ever saw me going to the extreme.

On March 15th, I called the agency and talked with a woman whom I will refer to as Joan. I asked her, "Is there any possible way that you can find my birth daughter and tell her that she has a file? I am not trying to interrupt her life, or to claim my rights as her birth mother. I just want her to know she has a file, and that I'm open to contact if she is."

To my astonishment, they said it was possible but they could not guarantee anything. If I was willing to pay the $100 fee and fill out some forms, then they would see what they could do. One hundred dollars seemed cheap to me. I would have paid any amount to make it possible for my daughter to find me! I didn't ask how long this might take. Assuming that the process would take months, I wasted no time filling out the form and paying the fee. On March 22nd, only one week later, I drove to market to help my husband with our produce stand in Reading, Pennsylvania. Mom was at my house caring for all four kids, and getting them on the school bus. She called me at market and said, "Anita, I just received a call from Joan at the adoption agency. She wants you to call her. They've found your daughter."

When we hung up, I thought my heart would beat out of my chest. Tears flooded my eyes, and my hands trembled as I dialed the number for the agency. For 21 years she'd been like a fantasy in my mind. Someone had found my birth daughter! In a few seconds I'd possibly know her response to my desire to meet her. Would it be what I'd hoped for or would I be prevented from having a role in her life? Would she open her arms to me, or close the door to a relationship?

When Joan answered the phone, her first words released a flood of tears. "Anita, we've located your daughter, her name is Twila." That was the first time I'd heard her name—her beautiful name: Twila. Hearing her name made her seem so real. It was all so amazing after all of these years. I now had her name but her face was still a mystery. Would I eventually receive that gift, too?

Joan told me that Twila was married, and had a one-week-old baby girl. I could hardly believe my ears! My daughter was already married and had a child? That meant that instead of finding just a daughter, I was getting a son-in-law and a granddaughter. God's timing in all of this was a miracle. First, I felt a sense of relief knowing she was married because that meant she was on her own, not living with her parents who might perceive our meeting as threatening. And second, now that she had her own daughter, maybe she could better understand why I had this desire to connect with her.

Joan said Twila was surprised to hear about me and her file, and that she wanted to talk to her husband, her parents, and his parents before she responded. She'd call the agency back and let them know if she'd like further contact. Even though I didn't know how our story would unfold, I was filled with wonder and joy. Could it be that I'd finally be blessed to meet my daughter—my own flesh and blood?

That was the longest weekend of my life. On Tuesday, Joan called and said that Twila had talked it over with her family and they all agreed it was appropriate for her to write one letter to me. Joan promised to call me as soon as she received the letter so I could pick it up. She offered to mail it to me, but there was no way I was going to wait a moment longer than I had to. For now, for the protection of both parties, all contact would have to be through the agency. There was no mention of how long it might be until the letter would come so I was left to play the waiting game. Every day, I waited for the phone to ring with the news that the letter had arrived. During this time, my heart started beating with the excitement of thinking I could possibly send her a gift through the agency. Having experienced the joy of giving my own children gifts increased my desire to want to give my birth daughter gifts as well. Here might be an opportunity to send her a gift from my heart. What could I send my daughter that would not be threatening, but that she would like?

With Easter just around the corner, I decided to send her flowers. This was my way to thank her for giving me the wonderful privilege of learning more about her. Since roses are one of my favorites, I went to the local florist and ordered 21 pink and white long-stemmed roses, one for each year of her life. I made sure that the woman who took the order understood that these had to be the nicest roses possible. When the sales clerk asked where to send them, I smiled sheepishly and told her I didn't have the address but that she could call the adoption agency and request it. As the woman called the agency and wrote down Twila's address I wanted to jump over the counter and see where Twila lived! But for now I would just have to hang in there and trust God's timing on that revelation.

Finally, Joan called two weeks later to tell me the letter had finally arrived. Dad drove to the agency to pick it up because I was working at the market that day. After work, I drove to my parents' house where my sisters met me. We gathered around the island in my parents' kitchen and dad handed me the letter. I was shaking like a leaf as I opened it. A couple of pictures fell out. After 21 years we were about to see our first glimpse of my little girl. They were pictures from her early childhood, one as an infant and one taken when she was six years old.

April 22, 1996

"Dear Diary: Two of my sisters were there. It was a very exciting moment in our lives. In fact, it was a moment I'd never visualized actually happening. We could hardly believe it. To get my first look at Twila as a baby and at six years old was a wonderful gift from my Lord. How can I

thank Him enough? I'm undeserving. Great is His mercy."

Twila admitted in her letter that the call from the agency came as a shock, and she was writing with mixed feelings. She felt she owed it to me to write and give me the assurances that I'd longed for.

Twila told me she'd been very happy growing up in her conservative Mennonite family in Pennsylvania. She'd been raised in the same county in which I lived! I had assumed that she was given to a family in another state. She went on to tell me, to the credit of her parents, she'd never struggled with the knowledge that she was adopted. She knew her parents loved and accepted her as their own flesh and blood. She wrote:

> *From as early as I can remember, mother assured me over and over that I came to them, not because you didn't want me, but because you wanted me to have a secure Christian home, and knew you couldn't provide that for me under the circumstances. She reminded me many times that God led us to each other, and this was His will for my life. And so, because of her influence, I've never felt rejected by you, or been resentful toward the choice you made. I'm extremely grateful to you for giving me to a home where I've known only love and security.*

Her words comforted me like no others. In that one paragraph God had proven himself faithful to that prayer I'd prayed 21 years ago in that tiny closet in my bedroom, "Please take care of my baby and provide a loving home for my child."

Twila ended her letter by saying that since she now had a baby girl of her own, she understood in a new way how I must feel about her. She wrote:

I'm sure it has not been easy to cope with your decision in the years since you placed me for adoption. I do not want to make things any harder for you. Rather, I hope that knowing something about me will help to heal your emotional scars and put you to rest . . . We trust the future to the Lord, and continue to pray for you and for wisdom to go from here. May God bless you!

Sincerely, your birth daughter, Twila.

[To read Twila's letter in its entirety, turn to "Reassurance from Twila" at the conclusion end of this book.]

Her response seemed so mature for a 21-year-old that I wondered how long it had taken her to write her letter! Had she reread and rewritten hers 20 times just as I had when I wrote my first letter to her? One thing I noted was her beautiful handwriting.

This personal handwritten letter immediately became a treasured possession. I couldn't read it enough. Every day I'd pick it up and read about her all over again. I wanted to know all I could about her. In fact, I still had no guarantee that I'd ever receive another letter from her, so I guarded this one with my life!

Now it was my turn to respond to her. As I sat at my desk with the stationery in front of me and a pen in my hand, I couldn't get over the fact that I was able to write my daughter a letter. Even though I didn't have her personal address, I could correspond with Twila. My heart was filled with joy and my eyes with tears as I carefully penned my thoughts. Although I hoped that she would want to continue in a written correspondence, I wanted to make sure that she felt no pressure for further contact. Her one letter had given me all the assurance that I needed about her well-being. I was very grateful for that and told her not to worry about my feelings if she was content to leave things as they were. I desired her and her family's happiness above mine.

As I sealed the letter and prepared to deliver it to the agency, new hope welled up in my heart. Even though I was not sure if she would choose to respond to this letter, I did have the hope that she would at least get her file. As I waited for further response from her, I was amazed by all the tears I shed. I was sure Paul thought I was having a mental breakdown of some sorts! I'd often ask myself: "How could something that had happened 21 years ago unleash such a flood of tears?"

I really didn't understand all the tears at that time but looking back I realized that most of my pain stemmed from the fact that I had chosen not to see my daughter or hold her. Surely the fact that I had not said hello or goodbye to her the day she was born played a large role in the loss that I felt over the years.

In addition to processing what my tears were about, I now felt it was time to tell Josh and Ryan about Twila. Although they were not as old as I would have liked them to have been, the odds were increasing that Twila and I might meet. The boys seemed to take the news in stride. At age nine, they were too young to understand the ramifications of it all. Grateful that all my children were now aware of this half sister, I was at complete peace.

May 14, 1996
"Dear Diary: With each letter I find myself getting a little more excited and hopeful. At this point I do not know what the outcome will be. Will we meet face to face and say, "Well that was a good experience," and leave it at that? Or will we meet and desire to get to know each other better? In my mind I picture me having a part in her life. I want to be able to visit her and her family. I'd like to be friends but who can know? Time will tell. I can't help but wonder what the outcome will be. I wonder if she thinks about me as much as I think about her."

CHAPTER 12

CONNECTING THE PIECES

You would think that after I'd waited 21 years to meet her, a few more months of waiting wouldn't be a big deal, but those four months seemed forever to me. It was a tedious process of writing letters, mailing them to the agency, and them forwarding my letters to Twila. Once she received the letter she would wait several weeks, write me, mail it to the agency, then I'd go pick it up. Back and forth we went.

Not wanting to keep my family in the dark, I would share each letter that would come. This was a new adventure in our family and I wanted them to be a part of the process as much as possible, as long as they had interest. I tried not to play it up too much, even though my heart was extremely delighted on the inside.

Although the letter writing process was slow, it actually helped us form our new relationship at an appropriate pace. Joan offered promising words, "Anita, all of this will work out nicely." Each letter I received gave me more faith that the day would come when we would meet; but how long that would be was anyone's guess. "Be still and know that I'm God,"[16] was my anchor.

Finally, the break came. God must have decided that I didn't need to be still anymore. Two months into our letter writing I'd given Twila my home address. I wanted her to be able to spy on me if she wanted to, if that would make her feel more comfortable meeting me. If anything, I was sure she would like my flower beds. Giving my home address of Washington Boro turned out to my advantage.

---

16 Psalm 46:10 (NIV)

Joan called one day. "Anita, Twila called and asked me to tell you that you no longer need to go through the agency. From now on, she and her husband Daniel will communicate with you through the Bishop of their church, David Wadel."

"David Wadel! What? You've got to be kidding," I thought to myself, "He's a neighbor of ours."

You see, David owned a chicken farm one mile down the road from our house. In the past, we had bought all of the eggs that we sold at our market from David, and now I'd often drive down the road and buy eggs for our family. How long had he known Twila? Could he be the link to meeting my daughter face to face? A surge of hope and excitement over this new development swept over my heart. In fact, I laughed over what appeared to be God's sense of humor. Of all the places in the world that Paul and I could have bought a house, we ended up one mile down the road from a couple who knew my birth daughter!

When I hung up, I immediately looked up Mr. Wadel's phone number and called him. I wasn't sure what to say; I just knew I would be talking to one more person who had some contact with my daughter.

"Well, David, I bet you were surprised to find out I'm Twila's birth mother," were the first words out of my mouth. In a kind and warm voice, he admitted that he was somewhat surprised. He told me that he and his wife, Ruth, knew Twila and Daniel quite well. They'd met both of them when they were house parents at the Bible school Daniel and Twila had attended. It had been at this school where Daniel and Twila had first laid eyes on each other. The Wadels had even been at Daniel and Twila's wedding!

Trying to piece the puzzle together, I asked David how he had made the connection that I was Twila's birth mom. He explained that Twila's father-in-law, a Mennonite pastor, had asked him on one occasion if he knew of any Keagys that lived in Washington Boro. David said he did. Further questions about the produce farm and our twin boys confirmed our identity, and David told him, "Paul and Anita are my neighbors." It was at this point that Daniel's father revealed that I was Twila's birth mother. Our worlds were slowly coming closer together.

As we wrapped up our conversation over the telephone, I asked if my parents and I could visit him and his wife and share what our intentions were for wanting to meet Twila. They graciously agreed and I felt an instant bond with this couple who would become my lifeline to Twila. A few nights later we sat in their living room and they listened intently as my parents and I shared our reasons for wanting to meet Twila. We assured him that we had no intention of coming between her and her adoptive parents; we simply wanted to meet her and hoped for a friendly relationship. Dad especially enjoyed getting to know David because they'd grown up in the same area near Chambersburg, Pennsylvania.

Before we left, David handed me a small booklet that would help me understand Twila's religious upbringing. He also gave me a church directory.

Once I got home, I read the booklet. I wanted to find out all I could so that I could have a better understanding of her upbringing. As I started thumbing through the church directory it suddenly occurred to me that since I now knew Twila's last name, perhaps I could figure out where she lived. By the process of elimination I determined that she lived in Elkton, Maryland. My motherly instincts kicked in and the next thing I knew I was calling directory assistance for her telephone number. Of course, I knew I couldn't call her, but just to have her phone number brought a sense of closeness. It seemed that the possibility of our meeting was becoming more and more real.

The urge to buy Twila another gift came over me as I wondered what I could send her this time that would give her a little more insight into who I was as a person. A book that I'd recently read that had inspired me was the autobiography of Oswald Chambers, *Abandoned to God*. Why not send that? I mailed it to her a few days later. It was hard not to send a gift for little Emily, my new granddaughter.

June 25

    "Dear Diary: I wish I could send something for Emily, but that will have to wait. I don't want to be overbearing. I'm waiting now to hear from Twila. She received my letter via Mr. Wadel last Thursday night. The Wadels are going to her house for dinner on Sunday. Should I send something, like a hanging basket of flowers? I'm going to record things now as they happen because I've an entire book to fill."

A few days later I wrote:

June 30

    "Dear Diary: This has been an exciting day. Yesterday I went to buy some perennials. I bought some for Twila. The Wadels were invited to Twila's for lunch today, and I wanted to send something along. After I bought the flowers, I took them to the Wadel's, but they weren't home, so I asked their son if he'd make sure David and Ruth got them."

The next morning I called the Wadels to make sure they'd received the flowers. They said the flowers were loaded in their car, and they were preparing to leave. As they drove by our house, they blew their horn. A smile broke out as I pictured them delivering my gift to Twila. I prayed for their safety as they headed for Maryland, and throughout the day I prayed that God would guide their conversation with Daniel and Twila and that His will would be done.

    It was hard not to be a little bit jealous of the Wadels as I thought of how lucky they were to be able to visit Twila. Maybe someday I would have the same privilege. I could only hope that for now they would at least bring back a letter for me. I always tried not to get my hopes up so that I would not be disappointed, but it was really hard. Surely, Twila would send a letter back with them. Waiting for the Lord's timing was so hard, but I knew that the Lord would bring about His purpose in His time.

Later that night when Paul and I returned home from a motorcycle ride, I spotted an envelope on our porch table that the Wadels had dropped off on their way home. My porch was such a mess that I felt a little embarrassed, but with four kids it's impossible to always have things picked up.

Hoping I'd find more photographs, I grabbed the envelope and looked for a quiet place to be alone. But everywhere I turned, there were kids. So I went to my bedroom and lay on my bed seeking privacy.

As I opened the envelope new pictures fell out! This time Twila sent me more updated pictures of herself. There was one when she was 12 years old, and one of her at age 17. She even included wedding photos of her and Daniel. There was a picture of her family, and two pictures of my precious grandchild, Emily. In one of Emily's pictures, I could see the basket of roses I'd sent them for Easter. Since I'd told the florist my story, I had hoped she would send the most stunning roses she could find. Believe me, she had! They were gorgeous! In her letter and pictures, I could see Twila's thoughtfulness toward me.

Twila had sent a nice card that had the words "Thinking of You" printed on the outside, and even that brought joy to my heart. I tried to figure out what our next move might be. Later, when David and I spoke on the phone we had a good conversation, and we talked about how Twila and I should meet for the first time. That night I wrote:

July 1

"Dear Diary: I really cannot wait until we finally meet. I think we will be so relieved—at least I will. This anticipation and build-up is a lot of pressure. It's all I can think about at times. It seems to me that once we meet, we can relax and enjoy developing a relationship. Hopefully, all anxieties will be relieved.

My fears are more with her parents. I'm afraid they don't like me already because I could pose a threat to either Twila or them. But as far as I'm concerned, that is an unnecessary fear. I so badly want this to be exciting for them as well. My prayer is that they'll view this as a positive thing in Twila's life.

I try to put myself in their shoes, and I'm sure I'd have the same concerns as they do. I love their family picture. What a happy looking family. I can't wait to tell my parents when they get back from California. They'll be as excited as I am. They'll love the pictures that Twila sent for them. She is so thoughtful.

In my heart, I know this will turn out to be a wonderful blessing in all of our lives. The Wadels are going to Elkton on Wednesday, so I want to get a letter together to send with them. This will be such a busy week. Not only do I have to work at market, but I have to teach adult Sunday School on Sunday. Lord, help me. I feel so overwhelmed. I feel the tears coming.

You know, I try to evaluate why tears come when I think of Twila. You'd think one could only shed so many tears. I'm thankful for tears. I've always heard that God invented tears for release when there are no words to express our emotions. All I can figure is that these tears keep coming because, number one, the hurt was so deep of placing Twila for adoption, the pain has never left and, number two, tears of joy because at last God is allowing me the privilege of meeting my first daughter. 'Amazing love, how can it be/That thou, my God, shouldst die for me.'[17] That song came to my mind: Amazing love, how can it be that God, in His goodness, would allow me to enjoy this new blessing in my life? Thank you, Father."

17 *And Can It Be That I Should Gain?*, 1738, Charles Wesley, *Psalms and Hymns*.

Yes, the pain of loss I felt was deep but I could accept it with joy because I knew that I had chosen the best life for Twila. Not only had I chosen to give her life but she had been a blessing to many others as a result of placing her for adoption.

Finally, the day I had been waiting for came.

July 5

"Dear Diary: Yesterday, Mr. Wadel called to say he has met with Twila and Daniel and that they're now ready to meet. My stomach started turning flip-flops, and my heart started to beat fast. I can hardly believe this is happening. He suggested Tuesday, July 16, at his home. We would all enjoy supper together. I think I gave Ruth the idea, and she must have liked it, because I mentioned I thought it would be neat to enjoy a fellowship dinner together after we meet each other.

Anyway, the date is set, July 16. I couldn't sleep last night because this is on my mind all the time. David told me that Twila is scared, and nervous, like me. That makes me feel better. I know there is nothing to worry about. God didn't bring His plan this far for nothing. Truthfully, this is so exciting because I know God is fully in control. I cannot wait.

Today I decided I needed a new dress for the occasion, so I went to Talbots®. I got a little carried away because I came home with four outfits, along with jewelry. I've never splurged like that before, but even Paul said I needed some new clothes. He'll be sorry he said that when he finds out what I spent! I spent so much that I don't even have the nerve to record it. Well, I know I won't shop again for two years, maybe three . . .

My parents returned from California. Dad came right over to get the pictures. They're truly excited as well. I sure hope I can handle this emotional roller coaster."

July 10

"Dear Diary: I am so excited that I can hardly stand it! Just got my first letter from Twila "direct." It is the best letter yet, even though all of her letters have meant so much to me. In this letter, I saw full acceptance, plus she does view our meeting with joy, as I do. Everything she mentioned in her letter lifted my spirits so high. Thank you, Father. Only you could have arranged all of this so beautifully. Tears keep coming to my eyes every time I think of this entire situation. Will the tears ever stop?

Twila is helping me to feel more at ease with her parents' feelings. It's really hard for me to comprehend how they must feel. I really do want to be sensitive to them. I know this has to be hard and difficult for them. I do feel badly that I've caused them to experience these feelings that they're having. I hate to be the cause of anyone's pain, and yet I must look at the positive side, and that is that I gave them Twila, who has brought them great joy."

CHAPTER 13

THE REUNION

July 15, 1996

"Dear Diary: I'm sitting here now on my wicker chair. Lightning bugs are all aglow around me. It's so peaceful out. Well, here it is, the night before I meet Twila. My stomach has turned a few flips, but I've asked God to keep me calm. I'm trying not to be so emotional about this. I don't want to have any expectations. Truthfully, I don't even know what to expect, but my hope is in God and His purposes. I wonder what Twila is thinking about now. I'm sure she is a little scared, like me. I want to really enjoy the moment, and really, I can't wait."

As I sat on my front porch that night, I could hardly believe that I was hours away from seeing Twila's face and embracing her after waiting 21 years. Not only would I finally be near her, but I would finally be able to shower her with gifts. It was all I could do not to go shopping for all the presents I'd stored in my mind over the years—things for her birthday, Christmas and just for fun. So, I settled for a few things I thought they'd enjoy: for Daniel, I bought a book containing a collection of photographs of farms in Pennsylvania and Maryland; for Twila, a book on roses, because I know how much she enjoys them; and for little Emily, a neat Noah's ark book. Paul brought home watermelons from our produce market for the Wadels and for Daniel and Twila. Closing my diary, I headed into the house and up to my bedroom. The hour was late and I knew that I needed to get some sleep but I had serious doubts that sleep would come. I felt like a child filled with anticipation the night before Christmas.

July 16, 1996:
"Dear Diary: I woke up, and tried to pretend that it was a normal day like any other day. I prayed that God would help me not to get sick in my stomach from nerves and that I could remain calm. And actually, He did. I was able to take my kids swimming, and we had a relaxing afternoon. It went pretty fast. I thought I'd be nervous all day but I wasn't. I felt God really answered the prayers of many people—all my dear friends were praying over this day, and He did definitely give me a peace. I was very relaxed."

I tried to pretend that July 16 was just like any other normal summer day. Promising to take the kids swimming, I worked hard to get my chores done so that we could spend the afternoon at our neighbor's pool. Time went by fast, although I kept looking at the clock counting down the hours until I would see Twila. At 3:00, I rounded up the four kids and we headed home for an early supper. Paul and the kids knew I was meeting Twila that evening but it was hard for them to comprehend what I was feeling. They were genuinely happy for me and wished me "good luck." After feeding the kids supper I showered and put on one of my new expensive dresses that I purchased for the occasion. Looking in the mirror for one last look of approval I headed out to my car (loaded with all the gifts and fruit) to drive the one mile to the Wadel's house where I would meet Twila. I wondered, "Has she already driven by my house to get to the Wadels?"

As I drove down the road, my pulse rate began to rise. By the time I'd reached the Wadel's driveway, the tears started coming. David helped me carry all my gifts into the house and let me know that Daniel, Twila and little Emily were waiting for me in the living room.

The door was closed, so I couldn't see them. The scene I had fantasized in my mind about our reunion was seconds away from becoming a reality. In a way it seemed like yesterday that she had been born yet in another way it had seemed like ages ago. It was almost as if I was dreaming as I walked to the door and turned the knob. My stomach was in knots due to a nervous excitement yet I knew that Twila and I had prepared ourselves the best we could for this moment. My prayer was that she would not be disappointed after opening herself to this relationship.

With great anticipation I opened the door. My eyes immediately fell on the daughter I'd never met. That sight is indelibly imprinted in my mind. She and Daniel stood in the middle of the living room with Daniel holding little Emily, who was about 3 months old. Emily just smiled, having no idea of the significance of that moment.

Twila and I immediately embraced and we both wept. Being able to put my arms around her for the very first time was an incredible gift from God. Time seemed frozen as we stood there and I was doing all I could to soak up the moment.

When we got past the tears, we sat down to talk. I'd wondered what we would talk about, but we had no problem at all. I was full of questions, and there was a natural ease between all of us, even Daniel. I felt immediate acceptance from him.

We had arranged our meeting so I'd arrive early and meet Twila without an audience. This was a sacred moment and I wanted it to be private. So, I invited my parents to come 45 minutes later. What a thrill I had watching my parents walk in and see their first granddaughter as well as their first great granddaughter! Although they'd seen Twila when she was born, I knew this was a joyful moment for them. After all, they'd prayed for her every day of her life. It was awesome to watch the expressions on their faces as they talked with Twila and Daniel.

Paul had opted to arrive after my parents. He had worked late that day and didn't mind arriving last. Even though he had been very accepting and supportive, this was a new adventure and slightly out of his comfort zone. His willingness to join me that night meant the world to me. I wasn't sure what all was going through his mind but he was his usual good-natured self and seemed very comfortable and at ease.

After his arrival, we sat down to a wonderful dinner. Ruth had prepared ham, buttered new potatoes, lima beans and corn—which happens to be my favorite vegetable—and homemade rolls. The food was fresh from their garden and delicious.

I'd so often thought about what our first meeting would be like, but I had never pictured eating around a large dinner table with friends and family. I could hardly believe that I was actually sitting beside my daughter, eating dinner together with her. It was hard not to stare at her. Sometimes I felt like pinching myself to see if this was all for real! Inwardly, I was talking to God and thanking Him over and over for allowing me this incredible privilege.

After supper, we walked down the long lane to the neighboring house. The Rudisills attended our church and had a beautiful flower garden. I'd shared with them the exciting news of what would be taking place next door to them and asked if they would care if we used their manicured yard as background for taking pictures of this historic moment. They were thrilled to be a part of this day. We took all kinds of pictures and every possible combination of family members.

My favorite photo is of my dad who is taking a picture of Twila, my mom, Emily and me—it's a four-generation picture. He is bent over with the camera to his face ready to take the picture while we are smiling at him waiting for the flash to go. As the sun began to set, we wrapped up the photo session and headed back the lane to the Wadel's house.

Next on my planned agenda was to surprise Twila and Daniel with the gifts I had so carefully picked out for them. I knew that no gift could make up for the 21 years that we were apart, but I wanted to express my gratitude to them for allowing me into their lives. They graciously received my offerings and then to my surprise Twila presented me with a beautiful cross-stitch picture in a frame. The picture was of a long stemmed pink rose with the verse Psalm 18:30, printed in cross-stitch, "As for God, His way is perfect."

Did she really believe that? Had she not been hurt in the process of my placing her for adoption? Surely there had been times that she felt I had rejected her. God used the picture in my mind of her stitching that verse on the fabric to bring comfort to my heart. Her thoughtfulness in giving this gift was confirmation that God had indeed been faithful. Choosing to go God's way by giving her life and allowing Him to work out a perfect plan for both of us had been the best way for us to go! His way was always perfect.

Twila also brought a photo album she'd put together for a ninth grade school project. It was her autobiography told in the form of pictures and she told me I could borrow it for as long as I wanted. It was like receiving a prized possession—a window into her growing up years. I couldn't wait to take it home and study it leisurely, to soak in what I could of her younger years. With today's open adoptions, a birth mom has the opportunity to receive updates of her child but in the good ole days there was no such thing. All I had during those 21 years was my imagination and three notes from the adoptive mother that had been placed in my file.

As I had contemplated how our evening would end a few nights earlier, I could only think of praise and adoration to a God who had reached down in my loss and brought redemption to the difficult choice I had made so many years ago. How could I adequately express my desires to Him? Why not end the evening with prayer? I loved the idea, but the thought of praying out loud in front of strangers was a little intimidating. Surely, I would not be able to speak my true heart under such emotional circumstances.

I had always loved how King David expressed his soul to God in the Psalms and other passages of Scripture, so right then and there I decided to write a prayer of praise and thanksgiving based on the Holy Scriptures. I opened

my Bible and went to every prayer that had ever spoken to
my heart and began to piece together on paper words that
I felt adequately expressed what was deep in my soul.
When I was done, I carefully folded the paper in half, not
knowing if I would have the nerve to read it or not at the
closing of the evening.

As we were preparing to say our goodbyes, I worked up
the courage to tell them I had written a prayer that I was
hoping I could share as we parted, if they were all
comfortable with that. After reading their church's
doctrinal handbook, I knew that it was not the practice for
women to pray out loud, at least in front of men. I wanted
to be sensitive to their beliefs. The men graciously
consented and so our amazing evening together ended
with this prayer.

"Father, I come to you tonight to give thanks to your
Holy Name, for you are God. You are great and worthy of
praise. Splendor and majesty are before You. Strength and
joy are in Your dwelling place. We ascribe to You today the
glory due Your name and we worship You in the splendor
of holiness. Let the heavens rejoice and the earth be glad.
Let the sea resound and all that is in it, let the fields be
jubilant, and everything in them. We give thanks to You for
You are good and Your love endures forever.

"Today, I'd like to thank you for the wonders You have
done in bringing Twila back into my life, and not only Twila,
but Daniel, Emily, and their extended families. Had we
known then what we know now—that we would be
reunited 21 years later—perhaps the pain of giving her up
would not have been so great. Yet the loss I've known all
these years was bearable because of Your grace.

"You carried me over the years and often reminded me
that You experienced greater pain giving Your only Son to
die for my sins.

"Not only Your grace but Your Word and its promises
carried me through the deep valley of grief. Your promise in
Romans 8:28, that all things work together for good to those
who love You and are called according to Your purpose,

always gave me the confidence that You are in control. It was this promise that carried me through the nine months of pregnancy, the signing over of my legal rights to Twila, and these past 21 years without her.

"I thank you, for today I am realizing the fulfillment of this promise. Though I never knew her as my own, I thank You for the blessed gift of meeting her today. You are faithful, God; and Your compassions never fail; they are new every morning. You are good to those who seek You and place their hope in You.

"I thank you for being Twila's Heavenly Father and for providing her with godly parents who've nurtured and cared for her in a way I was unable to. Thank You for using Twila's life to fulfill their dreams of having a child of their own. I pray that they may know Your peace in the days ahead. May they know and feel in their hearts the assurance that Twila belongs to You first, to them second . . . thank You for Joan, who was instrumental in beginning the process of Twila's and my reunion. Thank You for the support and gentle encouragement she gave us. I pray that in some way you'll use the letters we've mailed through the agency to point her to You, that she may know there is a God who cares about every detail of her life.

"Father, thank You for Daniel's parents, particularly his father who was brave enough to talk to David, which led to the discovery that we were neighbors. Thank You for the positive influence they have been in Daniel and Twila's life. I thank You for David and Ruth and what they have meant to all of us. There are no coincidences! Only You could have planned all of this. It is because of them this reunion has occurred with much joy and excitement. They are Your faithful servants. May their lives be richer as a result of this experience.

"I thank You for my parents who stood by me during the difficult days. They could have been embarrassed and ashamed, yet they forgave me and helped carry the burden. Thank You for their godly example, support, and care over the years. I thank You that they're able to experience this moment with me and see the results of their faithful prayers.

"Lastly, I thank You for my husband, Paul, who has always loved me and supported me even though it was hard for him to understand my emotions these past months. Thank You that You brought him into my life.

"Now Father, we look to You and Your strength. Your word says that if any man lacks wisdom, he should ask God, so today I ask for wisdom and understanding for Twila and myself as we go from this point. This is new to us and we don't want to hurt family members on either side as we establish this new relationship. We ask for Your guidance and we place ourselves into Your hands. We know that You will continue to work out Your perfect will.

"Now to Him who is able to do immeasurably more than all we ask or imagine, according to His power that is at work within us, be the glory in the church and in Christ Jesus throughout all generations, forever and ever! Amen."

As we said our goodbyes, I wondered what would be next. Would Twila want to see me again? It was her call. I could only hope and pray that she would choose to let me be part of her life in the future.

CHAPTER 14

BECOMING MY DAUGHTER'S FRIEND

As Daniel, Twila and Emily prepared to drive home that evening, she pulled me aside and explained that she and Daniel had discussed further contact with me before our meeting, and they had decided it would be best for us to take matters slowly. Six months from now, we could connect again. Instantly, my joy turned to disappointment.

Six months? How could I possibly wait that long? I hoped my disappointment didn't register on my face. Yet, the Lord reminded me that just having the opportunity to meet Twila was a gift, and that I should be thankful for that. So I graciously accepted their wishes, gave them all hugs goodbye, and watched them drive down the gravel farm lane. It would be a long time till I saw her again, or so I thought.

Returning home that evening my kids were waiting up to find out how the evening went. I told them how "cool" it had been to see Twila and that someday they would get to meet her, too. After tucking them all in bed, I pulled out my journal and recorded my overall thoughts about my first impressions of Twila.

"Dear Diary: Twila is beautiful. I think our personalities are somewhat alike. She is very thoughtful, caring, and kind, and she seems to have a wonderful sense of humor. Daniel, her husband, is a gem. He was so relaxed about it all and very supportive. Good looking, sense of humor, fun. They really do make a neat couple.

*Emily is precious. It's hard to believe that I sort of
have a granddaughter."*

Several weeks later, I received a letter from Twila. She
had included a picture of us from our reunion. My heart
leaped for joy as I read that she and Daniel had reflected on
their earlier decision to wait six months before we would
see each other again. That seemed a bit unrealistic and, to
my delight, she invited me to visit her and Daniel in their
home. This was the best news I could have received!

On August 19, 1996, I received another surprise—my
very first phone call from Twila! As we talked, I couldn't get
over the fact that after all these years she was now just a
phone call away. This was an incredible privilege I vowed I
would never take for granted. I had admitted in an earlier
letter that I was afraid to make the first call, so I was
touched by the fact that she broke the ice and called me.

Twila and I didn't have any instruction book to tell us
how to build this new relationship as a birth daughter and
birth mom. Where do we go from here? How should this
relationship look? We decided that we would have to trust
God's leading, and take it one day at a time. We discussed
how she should address me. Although I was her birth
mother, it wasn't important to me that she call me "mom,"
because I was not her "real" mother. So I invited her to call
me "Anita" and I gave her the freedom to decide how she
wanted Emily to address me.

A few weeks later, I drove to Maryland for my first visit
in their home. I was now within an hour's drive and the
thrill of being able to get in my car and drive to see my
daughter was beyond words. The time passed quickly as I
relived our first and only visit. As I pulled into her
driveway there was still some anxiety. Does she like me?
What will we talk about? Is she really comfortable with our
new relationship? My encouragement came from the
knowledge that we both were women who had faith in
God, and believed the promises in the Bible. How could
this *not* work out?

> *For I know the plans I have for you, declares*
> *the Lord, plans to prosper you and not to harm*
> *you, plans to give you a hope and a future.*[18]

Twila and Emily greeted me at the door and helped to carry in produce from our farm and more gifts for their family. Daniel came home for lunch and we enjoyed sitting at the dining table, learning more about each other. Emily kept us well entertained, as you can imagine any six-month-old would. Daniel's parents also dropped by. I was thrilled to meet anyone connected with Twila. Daniel's parents expressed genuine gratitude when they told me, "Thank you for not having an abortion. Twila has brought Daniel and our family so much joy!" They could not imagine life without her and were thankful that I had chosen life for my unborn child.

In a few short weeks, I'd be meeting Twila's parents. I had seen pictures of them, but the thought of meeting them face to face was truthfully scary! One part of me could hardly wait to meet this special couple the Lord had chosen to raise my daughter. The other part of me felt nervous and afraid. Would they resent that I had interfered with their home life? Would they feel threatened by Twila's and my relationship? I tried to put myself in their shoes and in so doing I realized that they probably had mixed feelings about meeting me, as well. Surely, they had to be a little bit curious about me.

One morning as I was cleaning my house, I decided to call Twila. During our conversation she mentioned that her dad would be the auctioneer at a fire hall near Farmersville, where she grew up. My curiosity was aroused and a plan was spawned. "Hmm . . . why couldn't I drive to the auction and 'spy' on her dad? You know—see what he looks like, hear how he sounds. He'd never know who I was, since he hadn't even seen a picture of me. Maybe that would help me relax a little more about meeting him and his wife." Now I knew this was a bit sneaky, but what harm

---

18 Jeremiah 29:11 (NIV)

could possibly come from this little adventure? It would be cool to see her dad in his working environment.

Of course, I didn't dare mention this idea to Twila because I did not want to alarm her. Besides, I didn't know if I'd get all my work done in time to make the trip to Farmersville.

When we hung up, I went into overdrive to finish my housework. The more I thought about the idea, the more excited I got. One of my personality flaws is that when I get an idea, it is hard for me to let go of it. This was no exception. I showered and carefully chose my outfit. Since this was a daring escapade, I decided to dress accordingly. My skirt was khaki, safe enough, but then I put on a bright red blouse, a red belt and red shoes. As I got in my car and headed toward the auction, I wondered to myself, "What in the world am I doing?" As a stay-at-home mom, this was possibly the closest I'd ever get to a *Mission: Impossible* adventure!

It was a 40-minute drive through part of the most beautiful Amish country around! Horse-drawn buggies and their Amish drivers shared the back roads with me. When I finally arrived at the fire hall, the parking lot was filled mostly with Amish buggies. "Oh no," I thought, "I'm going to stick out like a sore thumb in this crowd! Twila's dad will surely notice me among all these plain dressed people." My adventurous spirit was shrinking, but I'd driven too far to turn back now, so I parked my car and walked to the entrance feeling very conspicuous in my bright red attire!

When I entered the fire hall I tried to blend in with the crowd, which was obviously going to be impossible. However, in no time at all I picked out Twila's father from the couple of pictures I'd seen of him. I spotted him near the front of the building talking with other visitors. He was just the kind of dad I'd have pictured for Twila—very personable, warm and friendly. I liked his smile. Not wanting to stare at him for long periods of time, I diverted my attention to a Noah's ark figurine that had caught my eye, thinking I would like to have that for my office to add to other Noah's ark paraphernalia that I enjoyed collecting.

As I stood there admiring it, I felt someone standing close. In a whispering voice I heard, "Anita, what in the world are you doing here?" When I looked up, Twila was standing right beside me! It had never occurred to me that she would've driven from her home in Maryland to the auction. Me? I felt like a little kid who had just been caught with her hand in the cookie jar! My red face now matched my belt and shoes!

She explained that her family was there as well as some of her relatives, none of whom knew that she had met her birth mother. We both started laughing at the whole scenario. I'm there spying on her dad, she catches me, and none of her relatives, looking at her, know that the woman in the bright red clothes, standing beside her, is her birth mother!

Knowing that so many of her relatives were there, I decided it best not to stick around too long. That was just a little too adventuresome for me! Besides, I'm a mom, and moms are smart. They have that sixth sense thing working for them. I suspected that Twila's mom had already spotted me and figured out who I was. Daniel and Twila walked outside behind me to say their goodbyes and then I headed to my car for the long drive home. At least I had seen her parents. Maybe that would help me to feel a little more relaxed about our first meeting.

A few weeks later I *officially* met Twila's parents in their home where she grew up in New Holland, Pennsylvania. It was rather astonishing to see how close she lived to me all of those years. In fact, there was a furniture store down the road from her house where I shopped occasionally. Just think, I could've been shopping in that very store while my daughter was down the road playing outside! That thought blew me away because of the assumption I had made over the years that she lived in another area.

As I pulled into her parents' driveway, Twila walked out to meet me. She probably sensed that I was a little nervous about the meeting. We walked together up the walkway, and were met by her mother. She and I embraced and the tears cascaded down our cheeks. Even in this awkward moment I felt bonded to this woman who had loved and cared for my birth daughter all those years.

Next, I met Twila's father. He was as warm and loving as I'd guessed, observing him at the fire hall auction earlier. We moved to the living room where we sat and got acquainted. As we talked, I sensed the pain that this reunion had caused them. They, too, had processed a lot of mixed feelings about Twila and me. Both expressed gratitude that I had not chosen to have an abortion and thanked me for the gift of Twila's life.

With tears in his eyes, Twila's father spoke. "Twenty-one years ago, you brought us great joy when Twila came to live with us. We know that you experienced a lot of pain over those years. It's now your turn to have the joy of meeting and being with her, and our turn to experience the pain of being reminded that she is not our own flesh and blood, although we'll always love her as our very own."

His honest expression was difficult to hear, yet our mutual love for Twila seemed to instantly bond us. Even though our first meeting was somewhat uncomfortable, I felt their warmth, transparency, and genuine acceptance. Seeing Twila in her childhood home and spending time with the parents God had chosen for her brought a closure to the mystery of her upbringing.

As I drove home that afternoon, I praised God for caring for my daughter in such a wonderful way for all these years. Yes, I'd missed out on her first 21 years, but now I'd have the rest of my life to enjoy her and her extended family. Our family circle had grown considerably larger!

November 1996

"Dear Diary: Twila brought me a Thanksgiving card. As I read it and treasured every word of it, I wondered if she could ever know or comprehend how every little thing she does brings me such joy. Tears still come to my eyes even now because I feel so blessed to have the opportunity to

*know her. I know God has helped me to accept
that she does not belong to me but my heart still
feels the pain of not being her mother. In one sense
'finding' her had been more painful than I
imagined. Yet, the joy of seeing her and being
with her outweighs the pain. She played the piano
for me tonight. She loves hymns—how happy I'm
to see her love for our Heavenly Father. God is so
FAITHFUL!"*

Yes, God was faithful, and I could not wait to start
sharing the long-awaited answers to my prayers with those
around me. I felt like King David who exclaimed in the
Psalms, "Since my youth, O God, you have taught me, and
to this day I declare your marvelous deeds. Even when I am
old and gray, do not forsake me, O God, till I declare your
power to the next generation, your might to all who are to
come. Your righteousness reaches to the skies, O God, you
have done great things. Who, O God, is like you?"[19]

I began to exclaim His marvelous deeds to all around
me, to anyone who would listen—from the church people
of the congregation I was a part of during that painful
experience, to college friends and acquaintances.

Now that Twila and I had met, and established a
relationship, I would have the privilege of keeping in touch
with her and would work at cultivating a friendship. After
all those years of separation, I could now just pick up the
phone and call her. I have since treasured every gift, card,
and letter she's ever sent me. Just saying her name brings
me joy.

Even the doctors who had been involved in my prenatal
care were not exempt! Every year when I had a routine
check up, I would keep them up-to-date. Dr. May had
recorded the following notations in my medical records:

> *We did discuss the child that she adopted out
> in 1975. She was very grateful to Alistair and for*

---

19 Psalm 71:17-19 (NIV)

the way that was handled. She has since gotten in touch with her daughter who she delivered at that time, has met her on several occasions and it has worked out to be a blessing in that they both have experienced joy as a result of meeting and developing a relationship.

Yes, joy was the perfect word to sum up our relationship!

CHAPTER 15

OPENING GOD'S FILE
FOR YOU

> *The God who made the world and everything in it is the Lord of heaven and earth and does not live in temples built by hands. And He is not served by human hands, as if He needed anything, because He himself gives all men life and breath and everything else. From one man He made every nation of men that they should inhabit the whole earth and He determined the times set for them and the exact places where they should live. God did this so that men would seek Him and perhaps reach out to Him and find Him, though He is not far from each of us.*[20]

My beloved friend, we are God's children and He has given us life and breath and everything else. God has placed us on this earth at this time in the exact place where we live so that we might seek Him, reach out for Him and find Him, though He is not far from any of us. Not only has He given us life but He's given us a File full of His own personal love letters, the Bible. The reason I put letters in my daughter's file is the same reason He has put letters in our File. He wants us to find Him, to understand how much He loves us, and to let us know how much He desires a personal relationship with each one of us. But you see He can't make us open The File. We must choose to open it.

Having done all He could to give us a File, it grieves His heart when we do not open it. I know that hurt in a small

---
20 Acts 17:24-27 (NIV)

way after personally feeling what it was like to have a file for my daughter but not being able to make her open it. Do you want to know why it is so painful? It's because you have so much love for that child that you feel you're going to explode inside if you can't show it! Listen, our Heavenly Father's love for us is so intense, and He longs for such a deep intimacy with us, that it crushes His heart when we choose not to receive His love. In a sense, refusing to open His File is similar to refusing His love.

Not only does He long for this intimacy with us but His arms are loaded with presents for all His children. In the same way that I longed to give Twila gifts but couldn't until she opened her file and sought me out, so your heavenly Father is longing to share His gifts with you. Yet we continually block the flow of those gifts by rejecting His love letters. And just as I was willing to pay any price to the agency to find my daughter, so God paid the highest price by coming to this earth in the flesh of Jesus Christ to lay down His life for you and I, so that we might experience true eternal life right now and in eternity through the presence of His Spirit within us.

If you have never taken the first step in receiving this gift, it is as simple as repeating this simple prayer:

> *"Dear God, I am a sinner. I am sorry for all my sins, especially that of substituting things and people in place of You in my life. I desire to come back to You and to turn away from this empty lifestyle. Thank You for sending Your Son, Jesus, to pay for my sins with His blood. I want to receive Jesus Christ as my Savior and confess Him as my Lord. From now on I want to follow Him. In Jesus name I pray, Amen."*

Another gift He has for us is His joy. Spending time reading his His love letters puts us in His presence and that brings a joy like you've never known! Every letter I received from Twila brought joy to my heart, because I just wanted to know her, and every letter revealed something new about her. Every time you read one of the letters from God you learn something new about Him and it can't help but bring joy into your life!

On top of all of these gifts is the miracle that we can really know Him. Jesus, in a prayer to His Father in John 17:3 (NIV) said, "Now this is eternal life; that they may know you, the only true God, and Jesus Christ, whom you have sent." (John 17:3 NIV). If Jesus says we can know God and Himself then it must be true! How incredible is that! Just as Twila and I learned to know each other through reading each other's letters, so we too can learn to know our Heavenly Father as much as we want just by reading His letters. The depth of our knowledge of Him is totally up to us. Believe this wonderful news, my friend. You can know God!

But more than wanting to give us gifts, He wants to prepare us for spending eternity with Him. In the same way that Twila and I prepared for our long-awaited reunion by exchanging letters we too must prepare for the day when we take our final breath and death comes knocking on our door. If we have spent our time here on Earth communicating with our Father through reading His letters and talking with Him in prayer then we will be well prepared to walk through that door and see His beautiful face without fear. The more time we spend learning all we can about our Heavenly Father, the grander the reunion will be! Wouldn't you rather be excited about your death than dreading it?

One last thing I want to leave you with. Never take His letters for granted. Every letter I received from Twila was a gift that I cherished. When I received my birth daughter's first letter, I had no idea if I would ever hear from her again. So I read each word slowly, trying to understand her, to know her heart. I hadn't seen her but I knew she was real, and this one letter was all I had to give me insight into who she was. I read it carefully for glimpses into her life and personality and simply took her at her word. Every letter that I received was another incredible gift. How I cherished her words and longed for the day that I would meet her face-to-face. God awakened me to the fact that I hadn't held His letters in awe like I had Twila's, nor was I honestly longing for our reunion when I would see His face for the first time.

Realizing that I had taken His awesome letters for granted for so many years and now having a new understanding of why He had placed those letters in a File just for me, I cried out to Him asking for His forgiveness.

That day I was forever changed. Never again would I read the Bible as I had before—out of legalism. Instead I started to read His letters just to know my Father more intimately. Each morning as I met with God, I'd pick up The File, open a letter and read it, thanking Him for this incredible gift. I'd grab a journal and write at the top of the page, "What do you want me to know about you God?" and then I'd make a list of anything I could learn about Him. It was like going on a treasure hunt! To think that I held in my hands the very thoughts of God and that He desired for me to know Him totally wowed me!

Cherish God's Word. Read His letters for the pure joy of knowing Him, not because you *have* to, but because you *want* to! And here is a guaranteed promise. The amount of joy you desire to experience in your life will be directly proportionate to the amount of time you spend in His presence seeking to know Him. You will never find true joy in possessions, successes, or relationships.

Because I understand and know the pain of having an unopened file, I plead with you not to grieve your Heavenly Father any longer. Pick up The File and read every single letter. Treasure these love letters, take the time to read them. Read each letter with a listening heart and keep reading them until the day you see His glorious face. Because that, my friend, will be the ultimate reunion!

REASSURANCE FROM TWILA

This is the first letter Twila wrote to me. As you can see, she approached the relationship tentatively just as many of us approach a relationship with God.

April 8, 1996

Dear Birth-Mother, Grandparents, and family,

I am writing this letter to you in response to your request for contact with me. The case worker's call a few weeks ago was a shock to me, and I begin this letter with mixed feelings.

First of all, I want to assure you that my life has been a very happy one. I grew up in a conservative Mennonite home, and have wonderful parents. Much to their credit, I have never struggled to accept being adopted. They love me and accept me as their own flesh and blood. I am the oldest in the family and have 3 younger brothers, who are all adopted also. From as early as I can remember, my mother assured me over and over that I came to them, not because you didn't want me, but because you wanted me to have a secure Christian home, and knew you could not provide that for me under the circumstances. She reminded me many times that God led us to each other, and this was His will for my life. And so, because of her influence, I have never felt rejected by you, or been resentful toward the choice you made. I am only extremely grateful to you for giving me up to a home where I have known only love and security.

I am now happily married and have a daughter of my own. My husband has 3 adopted sisters, so he and his family understand adoption and relate to it as only the experienced can. I have been richly blessed.

I suppose you are wondering how I feel about having contact with you, and whether I am at all interested. That question is very difficult for me because it arouses so many conflicting emotions. My desire to meet you up to this point has never gone deeper than mere curiosity. I <u>have</u> wonderful parents, who gave me everything except their flesh and blood; I <u>have</u> a family where I belong, and so I never felt I needed to know who you were. I had no idea what kind of people you were, and what I would expose myself to by finding out. Even now that I know a little about you, and know you care about me, this is a <u>very</u> hard move to make. It would be much easier for me to leave everything as it always was. I'm not sure how to put all those feelings into words, but I hope you can at least partially understand.

However, when I think of this from your standpoint, I realize that to be fair to you, I cannot ignore your request. Having just had a daughter of my own, I understand in a new way how you must feel about me. I'm sure it has not been easy to cope with the decision in the years since you placed me for adoption. I do not want to make things any harder for you. Rather, I hope that knowing something about me will help to heal your emotional scars and put you at rest.

We, and both our parents, have discussed having contact with you. We all agree that a very low-key correspondence through the agency is the only thing possible right now.

Outside of the fact that I need time to cope and adjust, we cannot risk unsettling our younger adopted siblings by letting them know about my contact with you. They are too young to be able to handle it.

I am sending several pictures, 2 of me and 1 of my daughter, Emily Danette, at 2 days old. My parents are also sending a letter along. We trust the future to the Lord, and continue to pray for you and for wisdom to go from here. May God bless you!

Sincerely,
Your birth daughter,

Twila.

PS: Many thanks for the gorgeous bouquet! Roses have always been my favorite.

CLOSING WORDS OF ENCOURAGEMENT

TO THOSE WHO HAVE FOUND THEMSELVES WITH AN UNPLANNED PREGNANCY

Your life is not over! A new life has begun— your unborn child's.

Do not buy into the lie that the child you are now carrying is not a life. It is! As a new mother, it should be a natural instinct to protect that child. Your child's life is a precious life that God is now weaving together in a beautiful way. You must now focus on how you can give that child the best possible life when he or she is born. You must go to God and ask Him to give you wisdom and courage as you look at your options, knowing that any choice you make will be difficult. Along with God's wisdom, you can receive good counsel and support from a multitude of networks around the country that will help you and other members of your family through the decision process. A good place to begin if you are facing an untimely pregnancy is to contact Option Line, the national toll-free center, at 1-800-395-HELP (1-800-395-4357) or online at Optionline.org (email and IM available). Loving and Caring is another national resource committed to bringing healing and hope to teens, single parent's, and families affected by crisis pregnancy. They can be reached at 1-717-293-3230 or Lovingandcaring.org.

God may have put you in a place where, with His help and the help of friends and family, you can be the mother your child needs. If so—wonderful. Make the choice to keep your baby. Once you are sure that this is the best decision for you, your family, and your unborn child, then choose to trust God for daily wisdom, courage, and strength to face the challenges of being a single mom. He will provide for your needs and the needs of your child, including finding a godly, loving husband and daddy for your child.

If you are considering adoption

You might be, as I was, feeling too immature to take on the financial and sacrificial responsibility of motherhood. Maybe you have grown up without the presence of a father in your life and have experienced the downside of that. There is nothing wrong with the desire of wanting your child to start life with two loving parents. Today's culture makes you feel guilty for even thinking that thought. There's no shame in choosing to place your child in the loving arms of a childless couple. It will be one of the most courageous things you will ever do in your lifetime. Placing your child for adoption can be a positive experience for everyone when done through the proper channels. If you have already made the loving choice for life but need help to take the next step, there are many adoption agencies that can provide professional services for you and your family.

If you are considering an abortion

For the sake of your unborn child and your own emotional and spiritual well-being, do not choose abortion. Everywhere I share my story, I have women come up to me who chose abortion years ago because they felt it was their only choice – a lie that many women have fallen for. They still carry the guilt, shame, and emotional scars of that loss. These feelings are a consequence of this choice. They come naturally because deep down inside something tells us that it was a wrong choice. That "something" is God. The memory of your abortion may particularly come to haunt you when you have future children. Many remember the day their child died and wonder who he/she would have become. Carrying that weight through life is a high price to pay. There are many available crises pregnancy centers/clinics throughout the U.S. and internationally who can help you explore options so you can make an informed decision, one that is best for you and that you can live at peace with. Choosing life for your baby and/or making an adoption plan for your child are life altering decisions, to be sure. But abortion, a choice that promises to take care of "a problem," only leads, many times, to years of intense regret, guilt and shame, and another whole set of problems.

If you've had an abortion:

For many women who have chosen abortion as a solution to an unplanned crises pregnancy, the reality of what abortion is feels too painful to face. Post-abortion men and women may live in denial for years as a way to cope with abortion's deep emotional and spiritual aftermath. Invariably, that wall of denial begins to crack as the truth breaks through the defense mechanisms set in place to distance and protect oneself from abortion's wounds.

Abortion produces many losses, the obvious being the death of a child. But for many, the loss of self-worth, relationships, joy and purpose in life can also lead to despair. Grieving these losses is a necessary step to heal. Accept your grief as normal, rather than something that must be covered up or pushed away. Accept God's forgiveness as you acknowledge your part in the abortion. Psalm 32:5 promises, "I acknowledged my sin to you and did not cover up my iniquity. You forgave the guilt of my sin." God desires for you to walk in freedom from abortion's guilt and shame.

Recognize that you are not alone. Many others have been through abortion and their experience and understanding can help you recognize that there is hope and healing for your heart. Many Christian, life-affirming pregnancy resource centers provide confidential after abortion counseling for women traumatized by abortion, and would welcome the opportunity to walk with you on this healing journey.

If you've placed a child for adoption

Be confident in your decision and understand that there will always be those trigger moments when you hear or see something that reminds you of the difficult sacrifice you made. A wonderful workbook that I found helpful in processing my adoption experience is *The Journey of Adoption*, written by Anne Pierson, of Loving and Caring, Inc.

If you've been adopted

I encourage you to maintain a heart of gratitude that you weren't aborted. Thank God that your birth mother chose to give you life! Thank Him for your birth parents, whether or not you ever meet them. Thank Him for your adoptive parents who fulfilled the role of mom and dad in your life! Commit your heart to become the man or woman of God He created you to be.

To the adoptive parents I say

Thank you so very much for your commitment to your child. You are your child's parents in every sense of the word. I pray that God will grant you years of joy and pleasure as you reap from the investment you've made in his or her life.

To everyone

Your birth father, Jehovah God, has written and filed His love letters to you in the Bible. Never let a day pass without spending time with Him there. Discover who He is and what He's like. Get to know and experience His great love for you. Commit yourself to live every day for His glory!

Anita Keagy, founder of JoyShop Ministries, frequently speaks and delivers inspirational workshops at churches, spiritual retreats, schools, and other venues. If you would like to contact Anita regarding a future speaking engagement, please visit www.joyshop.org or write to:

JoyShop Ministries
PO Box 118
Washington Boro, PA 17582